## *AN AFGHAN*

OCCIPUT

STOP

CREST

WITHERS

MUZZLE

BOW

# THE DOG LOVER'S LIBRARY
### Edited by *CLIFFORD L. B. HUBBARD*

## THE AFGHAN HANDBOOK

*Brian of Kakashan*
*- Mischa*
*(Carloway)*

# THE DOG LOVER'S LIBRARY

*Edited by*

### CLIFFORD L. B. HUBBARD

A series of breed handbooks each written by an authority of general or specialist repute, and copiously illustrated with engravings, prints and photographs of important early and modern dogs. Each book is an up-to-date monograph on a particular breed or variety.

*Other titles include*

THE DACHSHUND HANDBOOK

THE BOXER HANDBOOK

THE STAFFORDSHIRE BULL TERRIER HANDBOOK

THE COCKER SPANIEL HANDBOOK

THE PEKINGESE HANDBOOK

THE CAIRN TERRIER HANDBOOK

THE WELSH CORGI HANDBOOK

THE SCOTTISH TERRIER HANDBOOK

THE MINIATURE POODLE HANDBOOK

THE ENGLISH SETTER HANDBOOK

and others in preparation

The famous " Zardin ", by F. T. Daws, 1909.

# THE
# AFGHAN
# HANDBOOK

GIVING THE ORIGIN AND HISTORY OF THE BREED, ITS
SHOW CAREER, ITS POINTS AND BREEDING

BY

CLIFFORD L. B. HUBBARD

NICHOLSON & WATSON
LONDON

First published in 1951

Printed in GREAT BRITAIN
by
LOVE & MALCOMSON, LTD.,
London and Redhill

# PREFACE

SINCE the Afghan Hound first came to Britain in real strength some thirty years ago he has steadily won his way into the affections of British dog lovers. In fact he has since then received deserved support from practically all of Europe and America. To-day, as I write this prefatory note, the first book on the breed ever to be published is about to be born. In the fullness of time this fact will become well known, of course, but what may never become history is the splendid co-operation behind the production of this book. It does not pretend to be a scholarly standard work, being merely a small handbook on the breed for those who are interested in it, but nevertheless I have experienced an almost embarrassing amount of interest in its production from Afghan lovers all over the world. Therefore, although I am proud to be able to contribute this work towards fostering a still wider interest in the Afghan Hound I am conscience bound to thank my many old and new friends in the breed for writing me of their experiences and for helping me illustrate the book with what I regard a really fine display of the best ancient and modern dogs in the breed.

Naturally you will understand that although many of those who know the breed best held out a helping hand to guide me through the perils that come upon anyone bold enough to attempt a first work on a subject, I still had to find much of the way alone: if I have faltered here and there in the chapters on the early history of the breed (and I feel that some parts are unavoidably incomplete) then I ask that you will be as tolerant of the work as a whole as you were of my many inquiries for statistical information and other matters.

During the twenty years or so that I have been writing on dogs I have come to know many of those people usually called 'leading lights' in various breeds . . . these important breeders do not invariably overwhelm professional authors with assistance or even encouragement, but I am proud to say that without exception every person of importance in the Afghan world has, as I say, really done a lot to help me make possible this book.

Thus those to whom I owe acknowledgment are too many to list here. But I will especially thank Mrs. Phyllis Robson, the president of the Afghan Hound Association and Consultant Editress of *Dog World*, Mrs. Marion Foster Florsheim, who has done so much to promote the Afghan in America, Miss Juliette de Baïracli-Levy, Mrs. Molly Sharpe, Mr. and Mrs. Tønnessen, who have fostered the breed in Scandinavia, Mme. Deckers, Miss Clara Bowring, and Mr. Gerald Massey. Institutions as such are I feel too often expected to help professional writers without ever a thank you, so I add here that some of the information that I have passed on has been kindly given me by the Kennel Club, the Irish Kennel Club, the Natural History Museum, and the National Library of Wales. Finally I think I have the support of all Afghan lovers in saying that the courage of the publishers in allowing me to include in the DOG LOVERS' LIBRARY series this book (on what is from a publishing point of view so young a breed) deserves commendation.

CLIFFORD L. B. HUBBARD.

PONTERWYD, 9*th September*, 1950.

# CONTENTS

# ILLUSTRATIONS

# CHAPTER I

THE Afghan Hound has been known in Britain for well over half a century, and for the past thirty years has never ceased to attract increasing notice, so much so that at the 1950 Cruft's Dog Show we were able to see a mustering of close on 100 actual exhibits. Indeed, bearing in mind the fact that the breed was not imported in any real strength until the 1920's the Afghan Hound has received an outstanding British approval.

The reasons are not really hard to find when we consider that physically the Afghan is a finely built animal with a proud carriage of head and majestic action, and that in character he shows great independence of thought tempered with a strong personal attachment to his owner, traits generally admired in any worthwhile breed. His fine topknot, bare back and heavily coated trousers attract still further attention, and I think that although we should always remember that it is the dog who carries the coat and not the other way round it is true that his long silky coat is still one of his major attractions. But on top of all that there has always been an atmosphere of Eastern romance and intrigue, and an air of mystery and excitement about him that has drawn us to inquire of him, and of his history, with more than a passing interest.

The demand for information on the beginnings of the breed has never been satisfied however, for very little is known about the origin of any of the Eastern Greyhounds, and what we know of the relatively modern Afghan is not a great deal. The breed is obviously a very old one but it is impossible on the evidence so far revealed to us to say how old. It is believed that ancient rock carvings and wall paintings in certain caves in the Balkh region of north-west Afghanistan represent Afghan Hounds of a type found in the year 2200 B.C., which would suggest the breed is well over 4,000 years old at least. I have not seen photographs of these carvings and so I am not relying purely on them when I claim the breed to be an ancient one . . . it is more than likely that some form of Greyhound is depicted in the Balkh caverns and I would expect to find the dogs rather like the other Greyhound forms appearing on tombs throughout the East and Near East. Perhaps someone will make an expedition one day and bring us back details of the rock pictures.

Certainly the best specimens of the breed have always been found in the highlands of Afghanistan and in consequence the Afghan has also been called the Balkh Greyhound. Other names for the breed are Barakzai or Barukhzy Hound, Kabul Greyhound, Kurram Valley or Kurrum Hound, and Baluchi

**Hound.** The reference already made to the rock pictures explain why the dog should have been named after the region of Balkh. Barakzai (meaning the son of Barak) or Barukhzy is the family name of the ruling sirdars of the country, and as the best dogs were naturally reserved for the pleasures of the royal rulers the breed was universally known as the Barukhzy Greyhound. Kabul is the capital town and the seat of the hereditary sovereigns. The Kurram Valley is one of the principal caravan routes for the tremendous trade between Asia and India, and in this region (which is immediately east of Kabul and Ghazni) there is a large number of Afghan dogs, though they are more of the lowland type than the heavier-coated hill type. The name Baluchi Hound is an obvious reference to the fact that the breed is also found south in the plains of Baluchistan.

I think it would be as well if at this point we get out our map of the north-west provinces of India and see just where the Afghan's home is. While I have already said the best dogs have always lived around the higher country it must be remembered that the breed is widely distributed right through the whole of Afghanistan. Afghanistan proper, that is, the Afghanistan to which we refer when we speak of the home of the Afghan Hound, is a mountainous country east of the Persian border, west of India, south of the Amu Darya (Oxus river) and north of Baluchistan. This area carries most of the western reaches of the Hindu Kush range, and quite two-thirds of it is really mountainous and much higher than our highest British mountains. But the physical Afghanistan stretches further, as far north as South Turkistan and as far south as the Arabian Sea, thus including all Balu-chistan. Varieties of Afghan Hounds are found in prac-tically all areas of this vast region, and in the posses-sion of almost all the tribes of whatever extraction they may be (Persian, Turk, Mongol or Hebrew). Natur-ally in so great a region the type of dog found varies according to the climate, diet, work and care it is sub-jected to. The dogs of the plains are for the most part lighter in coat, while the highland dogs grow a profusion of hair like that we see in our own Afghans. The higher the terrain the thicker the coats on the dogs, and so it is quite in keeping with natural laws, with the reports of travellers, and with the traditional breeding of these dogs by the ruling sirdars that the best dogs have always been found in the mountains of an area which roughly approximates to the triangle formed by Balkh—Chitral—Ghazni.

This area, including as it does the geographical back-bone of Afghanistan (the Hindu Kush range of over 12,000 feet), is also where the best specimens imported into Britain came from, an area which includes the capital Kabul, and the one-time capital Ghazni. The latter town, which is 7,000 feet up in the highlands, gave its name to the celebrated kennels of Mrs. Mary Amps who was one of the pioneers of the breed in Britain—but that is by the way, of course.

Before putting away the atlas we see south of Ghazni the beginning of the plains where pack dogs used for carrying merchandise are kept ever busy by the Ghilzai tribesmen who carry on most of the caravan traffic into India with the produce of Afghanistan, the famous blue lapis lazuli stones, dried fruits, wool, and so on. These lowland dogs are fairly well bred and

Plate I

(*left*)
A Meenah of Jajurh with
his Afghan Hound, 1813.

*Courtesy Gerald Massey.*

(*below*)
" Shahzada ", after a
drawing by R. H. Moore.

*Canis Dog Features.*

Plate II

" Moti ",
a daughter of the
celebrated " Zardin ".

*Courtesy Miss de Bairacli-Levy.*

" Fatima ",
Captain F. Martin's
bitch.

A photograph of
" Zardin " in
1907.

looked after and are quite distinct from the common pariah of the East.

## THE AFGHAN IN SPORT

The dogs of Afghanistan are put to other uses as well as the carrying of merchandise. The best and fleetest of foot are kept for coursing deer and gazelle, and sometimes even for wolf and snow leopard hunting. The largest (who are not quite as good at coursing as the medium-sized dogs) are kept as watchdogs, making excellent guards. It is possible that Afghan Hounds were even trained to fight each other as well, for the *Encyclopædia of Rural Sports*, 1839—40, tells us the Afghans 'delight in the fighting of quails, cocks and other animals, and encourage the combats of rams, dogs, and camels; they also delight in horse-racing'. (Incidentally the same work reminds us that Persian and neighbouring dogs have been trained for the hunt since at least 865 B.C., when King Hushing was reputed to be the first trainer of dogs for the hunting of animals.) There are also some Afghans who are trained for herd work, mainly with goats but occasionally with the Afghan sheep, those sheep famous for their tremendously fat tails from which the natives make a kind of butter. There is a breed of Sheepdog specially kept for herding the sheep and goats but this is not a very common breed; I think a few Afghan Sheepdogs found their way into Britain towards the end of the last century, and these did not always arrive under their own name, but that is another matter.

The Afghan Hound is a powerful dog and fleet of

foot, and so it is not surprising that he has been used in the hunting of wild animals for thousands of years. The Afghan nobles, from the ruling sirdars and the influential khans to the petty chiefs, have long enjoyed taking this dog out with them for the big organized hunts, sometimes with trained falcons as additional assistants. A favourite pastime of the sporting Afghan shikari is that of hunting and killing the snow leopard, and indeed this animal has come to be regarded as the legitimate prey of the Afghan Hound in his own country. For this end the Afghan is specially designed, with relatively long powerful limbs, deep roomy chest, tucked-up loins permitting a maximum reach of the hind legs when in action, feet peculiarly adapted to suit the rugged terrain, and terribly powerful jaws. Although a typical Greyhound (it is a pity the group name Hound is tagged on, all things considered), and therefore a dog coming from stock which hunted by sight, the Afghan uses his nose quite a lot when in the chase. He is truly a great hunter well able to track a spoor unseen until the time comes for the final sprint when he speeds after his prey with fascinating finality.

By the way, the reference made to the breed being able to track down and kill the leopard is no idle boast for it is a fairly common occurrence for a well-built Afghan to tackle a leopard alone. Indeed the Afghans now in Britain are descended directly from stock bred for leopard hunting, and although there may be more I know of at least two of the early importations who killed leopards themselves. W. D. Drury in his *British Dogs* (Vol. I. The Various Breeds), 1903, quotes Major Mackenzie (one of the first importers of Afghans into Britain) as relating . . . ' " Koosh ", the grandsire of the bitch "Khulm" (illustrated in *Practical Kennel Management*), alone killed a nearly full-grown leopard that was carrying away her dam "Mooroo II", when she was a pup'. Then there was that very courageous dog "Khan of Ghazni" (imported by Mrs. Amps in 1925) who was reputed to have killed three leopards in the Paghman hills.

## EARLY ART AND LITERATURE

While literature purely devoted to the breed is practically non-existent apart from short chapters in general cynological works and a few articles in sporting, natural history, travel, and dog-breeding journals, the representation of the Afghan Hound in art is even scarcer. I do not doubt that somewhere or other there are excellent and true likenesses of the dogs, but I have not seen them, nor any references to their existence. I am almost certain that artists have portrayed this breed for the hereditary rulers of Afghanistan, at least when the Afghan Empire was at its height. I should think, too, that the breed must surely have been incorporated into hunting scenes woven into the fine Turkoman tapestries, hangings made in the surrounding provinces of North-West India and Persia, and in Chinese ceramic art of the animal-loving T'ang dynasty (A.D. 618—906).

Related Greyhounds to the west and east have been represented in Persian and Chinese art, respectively, and so I should expect to find at least some art representation of the Afghan Hound himself. Doubtless his isolation in a mountainous terrain (and the best dogs, as I have already said, were kept in the most difficult part of the country) has had something to do with his not becoming widely known to artists of the outside world: hill breeds are seldom depicted in art in equal strength with lowland races. For representations of the related Saluki you need only study any really worthwhile general work on dogs to find dozens of references and reproductions: *The Book of the Dog*, 1948 (Nicholson & Watson), and *Dogs in Britain*, 1948 (Macmillan & Co.), even have long illustrated sections on the dog in art, by Hesketh Hubbard and myself, respectively. But, as I say, although there are numerous fine works of art which portray or include the short-coated Greyhounds of Egypt and Persia, India and China, I know of none which shows the heavy-coated true Afghan Hound. When more people take an interest in the early history of the breed and travel to Afghanistan to study it (as a few are doing while I write) perhaps we shall be able to fill the gap.

Miss Clara Bowring tells us in an article she published in *Our Dogs* that when she was the guest of the Maharaja of Jaipur she saw a fine collection of early Chinese sculptures owned by the Maharaja, one piece of which bore a marked resemblance to the Afghan Hound. It is more than likely too that the breed was represented in some of the exquisite hand-decorated gold and silver work made in Afghan Turkistan.

Illustrations of Afghan Hounds in books are interesting if only for the unfortunate fact that very often artists, authors and editors got the breed mixed up with Persian Greyhounds and other breeds. I had hoped to have found illustrations worth reproducing here in dog books published in India, but although my collection contains every work published in India (thanks to the kindness of the Maharaja of Pithapuram, who most graciously presented me with what volumes I lacked) I found not a single Afghan picture.

Mr. Gerald Massey, from whom I have bought many of my early dog books, has been kind enough to draw my attention to a work by Thomas Duer Broughton, *Letters Written in a Mahratta Camp during the Year 1809*. This book, published in London, 1813, shows in the coloured plate 'A Meenah of Jajurh' a native soldier with a small Afghan Hound, probably one of the dogs customarily kept in the military camps as watch-dogs. The plate is not in all copies I have seen since Mr. Massey drew my attention to it but where it is present the dog is coloured dark brown. In the copy in the Secretary of State for India Library (a perfect copy, of course) the dog is a Van Dyck brown with a fawn trace running up the brisket. The colouring was done by hand, so it may vary in some copies, but as I say I have not yet seen one other than a dark shade of brown. The original drawing was made by a native Mahratta, Deen Alee, and the etching by T. Baxter. I had the plate photographed and have reproduced it on Plate I.

Now the dog is small—very small at first glance. But the text of the book (which apart from mentioning French lap-dogs being carried by the Mahratta women does not mention dogs) tells us that such an archer soldier as is depicted belongs to a race of 'well-built men', so that the dog is not so small as at first imagined. Moreover, I should think the bow he holds is a hunting bow of about four feet ten inches, the arrows, headed and fletched for hunting, are very long, being about thirty-four inches, and so if the artist has drawn everything in proportion the Meenah is about six feet three inches and the Afghan about twenty-two inches at the shoulders. This Afghan was probably a smallish bitch, reaching to about the soldier's knees; in the plate the soldier looks about seven feet high with his tuft of curlew feathers stuck in his turban! The Afghan has a topknot, a typical body and legs, huge feet and properly ringed tail set in the "Zardin" fashion.

Edward C. Ash searched high and low for references to the Afghan Hound when he combed the vast stocks of the British Museum Library during his researches for his *Dogs: Their History and Development*, 1927, but drew blank with the exception of one work which he quotes: (Vol. I, p. 200) 'The Hon. Mountstuart Elphinstone, in 1815, in his *Account of the Kingdom of Caubul and its Dependencies*, writes: "The dogs of Afghanistan deserve to be mentioned. Their Greyhounds are excellent; they are bred in great numbers, particularly among the pastoral tribes, who are much attached to hunting".' I am afraid my quotation does not exactly agree with the supposed quotations I have seen in so many allusions to the breed, but that is purely because when I quote an author I do so *verbatim, literatim, et punctatim*—as I think everyone should.

I have found no further reference to the type until 1840, where in Vol. II of *Dogs*, by Charles Hamilton Smith, 1839—40, appears a suggestion that the type member of the Greyhound group originated in a region about the western ends of the Hindu Kush, that is, in Afghanistan. On p. 163 Smith writes: 'All these circumstances taken together, seem to fix the origin of the

Greyhound somewhere to the westward of the great Asiatic mountain chains where the eastermost Bactrian and Persian plains commence, and where the steppes of the Scythic nations spread towards the north'. He refers (*ibid*) to the 'powerful Persian breed' west of the Indus. Well, Bactria or Persia it is much the same considering the movements of peoples and fluid frontiers of the time. In any case, as Mr. Croxton Smith points out in his *About Our Dogs,* 1931, Balkh is the ancient Bactria, which in the seventh century B.C. fell under the dominion of the Medes, later to be conquered by Cyrus, who ruled over areas to the east where the Saluki had been domiciled since time immemorial. On top of that Baluchistan is practically as much Persian as Afghan, all things considered, so that we need not be unduly alarmed at the early references which ally the heavy-coated mountain Greyhound with the short-haired lowland Greyhound. Mr. Croxton Smith suggests that the Afghan is really an offshoot of the Saluki ; if the latter travelled east and north into the mountains of Afghanistan it would have been perfectly natural for him to develop a heavier coat as protection.

On the other hand it is just possible that the thick-coated type was the earlier of the two forms, and, like many of the ancestral types of dogs has become isolated and less known to the outside world than the increasing number of breeds developed from it in the course of time. In support of the latter theory there is the opinion of H. D. Richardson, in his *Dogs; Their Origin and Varieties,* 1847, where he claims (p. 31) 'The original Greyhound was unquestionably a long-haired dog, and the modern smooth-coated and thin animal, now known by that name, is comparatively of recent date. Of this we have sufficient evidence in the ancient monuments of Egypt, where, as well as in Persia and India, rough Greyhounds of great size and power still exist '.

I have a tremendous respect for Mr. Croxton Smith's words and regard him as one of the very few dog writers I can really trust to carefully weigh the evidence before him, and am therefore anxious to keep an open mind on the question of whether the heavy, or light-coated type is the older. However, after very carefully considering the fact that in most other Greyhounds the heavy-coated varieties have been satisfactorily established as the older ones I cannot do otherwise than subscribe to the view that the Saluki may well be a descendant of the Afghan Hound. You may sense that I am hedging a little in admitting my considered opinion, but that is because I do not wish to appear dogmatic: in taking on the task of writing this book I have to consider all the evidence available to me as well as to others, and whether the publication of a true summing up involves burning my bridges in categorical statement or not that cannot be helped. Anyway, I believe that while a breed may put on coat when taken to a colder climate, in the long run all dogs the world over gradually shed their protective clothing as the earth becomes warmer, and breeds domiciled in even the temperate zones will in the fullness of time dispense with their coats altogether. Since even the fifteenth century our own European long-haired Greyhounds have practically ceased to exist, with the exception of the Irish Wolfhound and Scottish Deerhound.

The next reference known to me is from A. W.

Hughes' *The Country of Balochistan*, 1877 (Baluchistan makes up the southern half of Afghanistan). The author says: 'Shepherd dogs and Greyhounds are greatly prized, and their pedigree is as carefully attended to by the Balochis as is that of valuable dogs in Great Britain. Greyhounds of a good breed are said by Ross to be procurable in the Makān province at Panjgur, and again in the Kharān district'. Note what Hughes says of the keeping of pedigrees, for this is most important in view of the rumours that flew about in the early days of the breed's arrival in Britain concerning indiscriminate breeding and so on. To know that in 1877 pedigrees of Afghan Hounds and Afghan Sheep-dogs were maintained properly is really good tidings. I have not seen the work by Ross although I searched carefully through several stacks of shelves of books on all the North-West Indian and Persian territories in the course of collecting material for this introductory handbook to the breed. To my chagrin and as the penalty for perhaps too diligent a search I found that Sirdar Ikbal Ali Shah wrote in 1928: 'Dogs are not allowed to come inside the house and their utility is confined to the gates to keep watch'. This may not really be so bad if it applies to the dogs of the low-lands, to those of lesser value.

A little earlier I mentioned that a number of authors have mixed up their breeds somewhat, calling the Afghan the Persian Greyhound, and the Saluki the Afghan Hound, and so on. Well in 1879—81 the first English edition of Vero Shaw's *The Illustrated Book of the Dog* was published: there is no description of the Afghan Hound in this book although there is a large woodcut (p. 239) of five typical members of the Greyhound group, one of the dogs being a quite decent Saluki described as a Persian Greyhound. However, following up every available record of allied Eastern Greyhounds in an attempt to find fresh news of the Afghan I next examined my copy of C. R. Sundström's *Handbok för Hundvänner*, 1891, only to find that the generously coated Persian Greyhound (Bild 27, p. 156) who encouraged me to believe I had found a passable representation of an Afghan under another name was none other than the Siberian Wolfhound lying in the foreground of Vero Shaw's woodcut! This magnificent specimen almost fooled me: after realizing that I had then to contend not only with Persian and Turkistan Greyhounds but Russian dogs as well I immediately became suspicious of every picture I found.

Once the comprehensive work of Vero Shaw had set the pace for other cynologists books which made more than a passing reference to the Afghan Hound began to appear fairly frequently. In 1894 Comte Henri de Bylandt's *Les Races de Chiens* appeared, and in this work we find several illustrations of Afghans. As I write I have by me the 1905 edition of this work, that having the text in four languages and carrying the title *Dogs of All Nations*. In Vol. I (on sporting breeds) on pp. 765—769 appear his descriptions on the breed in French, English, German and Dutch. De Bylandt unfortunately appears not to know which is which of the Afghan Hound and the Persian Greyhound so gives each article the double heading of ' Afghan Greyround. Persian Greyhound '. And the same happens with the pictures he reproduces too: p. 766 has for instance a quite good reproduction of the ideal Afghan and Persian Greyhound as painted by our famous

Arthur Wardle, and here the caption is quite wrong
although the dogs are easily recognizable . . . the Afghan
being about as good as the early Bell Murray dogs
imported into Britain in the 1920's. On p. 767 are two
other illustrations of Afghans: a head study of an
'Ideal Afghan Greyhound' from a sketch by Ludwig
Beckmann, and a reproduction of R. H. Moore's drawing of Mr. J. A. Whitbread's "Shahzada".

The drawing of "Shahzada" was originally published
in Charles Henry Lane's *All About Dogs*, 1900, and is
reproduced here on Plate I. The same sketch was also
published in another *Dogs of All Nations*, a book by
W. E. Mason, published at New Jersey, 1915, which is
an obvious plagiarization of the work of de Bylandt.
It may even have been in Conrad Miller's *Dogs of All
Nations* as well (the New York, 1903 work) for all I
know, but as I have not seen this book yet I cannot say.
It is just possible too that the same picture appears on
No. 34 of the American set of cigarette cards, 'Dogs of
the World'*, published by Goodwin & Co. *c.* 1885;
this was probably the first set of dog cards ever published. (The first British set entirely devoted to dogs
was the Cope Bros. & Co. Ltd. 'Dogs of the World', a
series drawn by Cecil Aldin about 1905, but this does
not include the Afghan.) So we see that the early
importation "Shahzada" was accepted as a faithful
representation of the breed in Europe, Britain and

---

* Since I wrote the above I have examined a set of these coloured
cards and I see from my article describing the set and identifying
almost all of the dogs portrayed in the fifty cards (I recognized forty-
four of the fifty), published in the November-December 1950 issue of
*The Cartophilic World*, that No. 34 was captioned ' Persian Hound '
and depicted an unnamed dog. The illustration has been published
in several foreign dog books, the earliest of which I can trace as yet
was Fitzinger's *Der Hund und Seine Racen*, 1876.

America, although to my mind the dog was quite a way from being the true Afghan of the Balkh—Chitral—Ghazni region.

## EARLY IMPORTATIONS

In dealing with the first few books featuring the Afghan we have had occasion to meet the dog "Shahzada", and it appears that this dog may have been given undue prominence because of the several publications of the Moore drawing. However, the Afghan in the Wardle painting was a far better dog: unfortunately I have not been able to get hold of a good enough photograph of that painting to illustrate the fact, but nevertheless if you consult the de Bylandt work you will see that the Wardle dog is much nearer the highland (the long-coated) type. "Shahzada" as you can see from Plate I was one of those obviously very thin-coated dogs common to the lower foothills of southern Afghanistan. Moore was an excellent artist, so I do not doubt the animal was almost as scraggy as in the picture.

This dog was first named "Gazelle" and won prizes under both names at various times. As "Gazelle" he shared a second prize at Cruft's Dog Show in 1895 with an Elkhound in the class for foreign dogs, but came third as "Shahzada" at the Chow Chow and St. Hubert Schipperke Clubs' show (Royal Aquarium, December) in the same year, being beaten by two Dingos. He had a better run in 1896 when he won a second at Cruft's, a first at the Pet Dog show, and a second at the Chow Chow Club show. In 1897 he won a first at the Pet Dog show (Royal Aquarium, May) beating another Afghan for the first time. On this occasion he beat " Dilkoosh " (who appeared in the *Stud Book* as an ' Afghan Bamkhzy Hound ') and a Dingo. But at the Kennel Club show in the same year he was beaten to second place by a Mexican Hairless Dog called " The Hairy King ". And in 1898 he won a first prize under Mr. J. Sidney Turner at the Kennel Club show (Crystal Palace, October), beating a Husky and a German Pointer.

Major T. Mackenzie and Captain Cary Barnard imported several Afghans towards the end of the century, the former being considered an authority on the breed at the time. His dogs attracted much attention. His " Khulm " was quite a good dog really but the illustration of this dog in W. D. Drury's *Practical Kennel Management,* 1897, is rather a poor one, and the copy reproduced in *Hutchinson's Dog Encyclopædia,* 1935, is even poorer. " Khulm's " grandsire " Koosh " was the dog who as I said earlier in this chapter killed a leopard which attacked " Khulm's " dam " Mooroo II ". A delicate drawing of the bitch " Mooroo II " (with " Mukmul ") appears in Drury's *British Dogs* (Vol. I, The Various Breeds), 1903, on p. 139.

Mr. W. K. Taunton was a fancier who was keenly interested in exotic breeds and who never failed to help rivet attention on any newcomer. As soon as the Afghan or Barukhzy Hound began to compete against his Huskies, Dingos, Hairless Dogs and other ' dog-oddities ' he obtained several himself, and was probably the first to exhibit an Afghan Sheepdog. At the Warwick and the Maidstone shows of 1884 he won prizes with the black-and-white "Khelat", and again at the Warwick show of 1888. "Khelat" has been referred to as an Afghan Hound but was really an Afghan Sheepdog, as the reproduction of the drawing by R. H. Moore in A. Croxton Smith's *Everyman's Book of the Dog*, 1910, clearly reveals (opp. p. 250). Shaggy, and with a docked tail, he is nothing whatever like an Afghan Hound, but very like an old-fashioned working type of Old English Sheepdog (the rather unbeautiful and not too tall kind seldom seen to-day).

The following year, 1885, saw another Afghan Sheepdog, the Rev. A. Carter's "Kushki" being exhibited. "Kushki", a creamy white, was born in 1881 and won a prize at the Kennel Club show in 1885.

But Taunton did have genuine Afghan Hounds as well as Afghan Sheepdogs and he showed a nice bitch called "Motee" at Bristol in 1886, where she won the first prize in the Foreign Dog class beating her kennel mate "Empress of China" who was described as a Chinese Edible Dog. Taunton's "Roostam" (pedigree unknown) and "Motee" became the property of Mr. T. R. Tufnell, who bred from them the famous fawn "Rajah II" in December 1883.

In 1887 another winner was "Mukmul", a dark fawn owned by Major T. Mackenzie. "Mukmul" tied with his fawn bitch "Moroo" for a second prize at Barn Elms show, 1887, "Moroo" then being four years old. "Mukmul" was rather like "Mustapha", who came to Britain with the Shah of Persia.

"Rajah II", son of "Roostam" out of "Motee", was bred by Mr. Tufnell and exhibited often by Mr. F. Carter of Carshalton, the first major appearance that

I can trace being at the Crystal Palace show of 1889, where he won an equal third in the Foreign Dog class with E. S. Woodiwiss' Hairless Dog "Zulu Chief". (Mr. Woodiwiss was the famous Dachshund breeder: see *The Dachshund Handbook* in this series.) "Rajah II" was considered quite a typical Afghan in his time, moreover he carried a slightly better coat than "Shahzada", and although having the typically wide hip-bones did not appear anything so gawky a dog.

In 1901 the body of "Shahzada" was presented by Mrs. Whitbread to the British Museum (Natural History) and this was mounted and placed on exhibition, where it is still on view to-day. The same lady also presented the body of an Afghan bitch in 1903 to the Museum, but what this bitch's name was I do not know; it might have been "Dilkoosh" but is not entered in the Museum register, and the senior experimental officer tells me that he has not been able to find the specimen itself! Certainly "Zardin" is not there, however many people may have said he is. By the way, I have often thought it is a pity we do not have in Britain a Cynological Society where a complete library of dog books and a museum of selected specimens of each breed could be preserved. The books in the Kennel Club library are not ordinarily available, and the mounted specimens of various breeds in the British Museum (Natural History) are for the most part of dogs who when living were not the best. I think if such a society could be formed it could 'book' its selected bodies in advance (as I have done when building up my collection of dog skulls) choosing really typical dogs. The Peabody Museum of Natural History, in New Haven, Connecticut, U.S.A., has gone a long way towards forming a representative collection of mounted specimens, although its habit of taking a skeleton or a skull where it cannot get hold of an entire specimen makes it rather an untidy affair, like that in our own Museum at Kensington where a breed may be represented by anything from a whole body down to a drawing of a head.

The next important Afghan to be exhibited was Captain Cary Barnard's " Afghan Bob ". This dog was brought from Peshawar in 1902 and was still not a full-coated Afghan. The best illustration of " Afghan Bob " appears in Robert Leighton's *The New Book of the Dog,* 1907, on p. 482 of both the fine edition specially prepared for subscribers and the ordinary thick single-volume edition.

On the same page in Leighton's book is also a photograph of " Fatima ". The picture was taken when she was at the age of eleven months and is fairly good as it has been retouched: I have reproduced on Plate II the original photograph with its background of palms and boulders because I prefer not to retouch illustrations unless it is really necessary. " Fatima " was owned by Captain F. Martin of the 25th Punjabi, at Rawalpindi. She is obviously one of the genuine mountain type, with the thick hair and topknot promising to develop into the full glory of an Afghan Hound's coat. This snapshot of her appeared (I think for the first time) in *The Illustrated Kennel News,* of 3rd May 1907 (p. 557), and on p. 555 of that issue was published a note on the breed in the column 'Echoes of Fancy'. To quote two passages: 'The photograph shows the thicker coat (which latter will probably get corded), the hair on the top of the head, and more powerful build of the

Plate III

Miss Jean C. Manson's
" Ranee ",
by " Rajah " out of " Begum "

*Canis Dog Features.*

*right)*
A group of Captain
John Barff's dogs.

*below)*
Four of
Miss Evelyn Denyer's
early Afghans.

Photo by]                                                    [*Country Life*

Plate IV

Mrs. Mary Amps' famous red dog
" Sirdar of Ghazni ".

*Canis Dog Features.*

Miss J. C. Manson's
" Buckmal ",
the first Champion
dog.

Mrs. A. B.
Willans'
" Shadi,"
the first
Champion
bitch.

*Courtesy
Mme. Deckers.*

Afghan, Barukhzy, Kurrum Hounds. . . . Our correspondent says that a friend of his who had lived in Afghanistan had never seen a dog like " Fatima ", but that proves nothing '; and, to quote again: ' The Afghan Hounds, like the ' Rampur ', are rather less reliable in temper than the Persians (though some of these are very nasty). It all depends on the bringing up '.

## THE FAMOUS " ZARDIN "

And now we come to the great dog " Zardin "; the Afghan who was destined to influence the future of the breed to the extent of becoming the accepted model upon which the official Standard description was based: " Zardin " the first of the genuine Afghans, full coated and full blooded. " Zardin " was imported from Seistan province into Britain by Captain John Barff in 1907, and came out of quarantine just in time for Mrs. M. C. Barff to exhibit him that year. Entered in a strong class (the Foreign Dog class again) with Mr. W. R. Temple judging, " Zardin " beat, at his fifty-second Kennel Club show held at the Crystal Palace on the 22nd, 23rd and 24th October 1907, all other entries including Captain Cary Barnard's " Afghan Bob ". The official citation runs: ' A.O.V. (in Foreign Dogs Class) 1 Barff's " Zardin "; 2 Cary Barnard's " Afghan Bob "; 3 Cust's " Minka ".' I do not give the full report of that particular show but if you wish to consult it it appears in the *Kennel Gazette* for Saturday 2nd November 1907, written by the judges.

On Plate II I have reproduced one of the earliest

photographs of this famous dog. It is one taken by J. Russell & Sons, and clearly shows the wealth of top-knot, coat and large feet, the dark mask and saddle, and the ring of the tail. Another photograph was taken by Coates & Co., of Bristol, and was published in *The Illustrated Kennel News* in 1907.

" Zardin " always attracted a good deal of attention and was never beaten at British shows. He had been exhibited at Quetta before coming to Britain. He was painted by Mr. F. T. Daws (together with a bitch named " Afghan Lass ") in 1909, and this painting is in the possession of Mrs. Phyllis Robson, the Consultant Editress of *Dog World.* By the kind permission of Mrs. Robson I have been able to illustrate " Zardin " in the frontispiece from part of this painting. This dog eventually became the property of Messrs. Shackleton & Co., a firm of animal dealers with premises in Leadenhall Market, London. Mr. Shackleton bought several Afghans from Captain Barff and bred from them. It should be remembered that Captain Barff had other dogs besides " Zardin ". The illustration on Plate III shows four similarly coated Afghans owned by him (who were all exhibited), and is taken from a photograph also published by F. T. Barton many years ago under the caption ' A group of Afghan Greyhounds '. On p. 751 of J. Sidney Turner's *The Kennel Encyclopædia*, 1907—11, appears an illustration above the legend ' Persian Greyhound (Puppy). By " Zardin ".' This puppy appears to me to be so much like " Fatima " that I think we can safely take it that it is her, and that therefore she was a daughter of "Zardin". The article in this particular book, which describes among other eastern Greyhounds the

Afghan, is by the Rev. H. W. Bush, who gives us two fine portraits of " Zardin ", both showing his typical proud carriage of head, good length of neck, and ringed tail not carried above the level of the back. (I do not see the proud head carriage, the springing gait and well-bent hindquarters of the real Afghan so often these days as I did in years gone by . . . it is a pity these points are not more concentrated upon by newcomers to the breed.) Of " Zardin's " tail, by the way, I think he invariably carried it below the level of the back so that the tip never rose in its ringed flourish to any point above the set-on ; his was never a truly gay tail (except in moments of excitement), although it was usually flown a trifle higher than in Mr. Daws' painting as we see it in our frontispiece.

The great " Zardin " was used, although I have never seen his name in any Afghan pedigree as yet (I doubt if it appears at all), and sired at least two litters, one being from a bitch also in Mr. Shackleton's possession. Of this litter only two puppies survived both of whom were bitches. These were sold to Captain Hamilton, the Dublin breeder of Bulldogs and Great Danes, but in September 1912, one was acquired by Mr. Norman G. Hadden of Porlock, Somerset. Mr. Hadden named her " Moti ", and the illustration of her on Plate II is from a photograph taken of her at the age of four months, and kindly provided by Miss Juliette de Baïracli Levy. In a letter from Mr. Hadden it appears that " Moti " suffered rather badly from a skin disease ; on the outbreak of the First World War she was given by Mr. Hadden to Mr. Styles, the Birmingham breeder of Great Danes and Borzois, but after the skin trouble had broken out again she had to be painlessly destroyed.

About this time all Mr. Shackleton's dogs died under rather mysterious circumstances and so it is extremely unlikely that any other British issue of "Zardin" (assuming there ever were any) lived to perpetuate his line.

To conclude this chapter on the history of the breed's very early days in Britain I feel compelled to at least mention another Afghan of interest, the dog "Baz" who was bred to a Greyhound bitch in order to give additional stamina to the Greyhound!

"Baz" was a red Afghan bought from a caravan in Baluchistan by an Indian Army officer, later the property of Mr. N. Dunn, the Northumberland racing Greyhound breeder. Mr. Dunn had a registered bitch Greyhound named "Explosion" (by "Father of Fire" out of "Ennis") and he put "Baz" to this bitch some time in 1911, and from what few accounts I have found of the experiment the puppies turned out to be quite fast and staying racers. Mr. Will Hally relates in *Our Dogs* (9th April 1937), that "Baz" (assuming this is the dog he meant, for at that time he could not recall the dog's name) was twenty-six inches at the shoulder and weighed sixty-three pounds. And in the 5th March 1937 issue he tells us that the progeny (who all had the typical Afghan ring to their tails) could not be registered in the *Greyhound Stud Book*. However, Charles Castle, the writer on Greyhounds, says (*The Book of the Dog*, 1948, p. 802): 'Mr. Dunn of Northumberland [was] by resolution of the National Coursing Club . . . permitted in 1911 to register in the *Greyhound Stud Book* "Baz", an Afghan Hound'. So that even if the progeny were not registered it appears that the Afghan sire was, although I have not searched the volume of the *Greyhound Stud Book* which contains the registrations for 1911, and cannot myself vouch that he was registered.

Breeders of 'Longtails' still have ideas about the usefulness of Afghans it seems, for a couple of years ago Miss M. C. Mathews (the 'Westover' kennels) related the following (*Dog World,* 21st May 1948): 'I was stopped a while back by a man who said, "Are you the lady what owns them woolly Greyhounds?" I admitted it. "Well, I want to use the black 'un to my lurcher bitch to put a bit of go into 'er pups". Having politely refused his offer of 5/- for 'yer trouble' I told him of a good lurcher. That evening "Ali" became restive. I was going to let him out for his usual evening stroll on his own, but decided to have a look round first; sure enough there was the chap and lurcher waiting for him; he evidently knew "Ali" came out about that time!'

But apart from stories of Lurchers the Afghan really can 'put a bit of go' into himself when running at full speed. Mrs. Molly Sharpe did in fact try the Afghan out on a proper racing track in 1937, where her string of dogs ran very well indeed after the electric hare. One of the Afghans tried out that way was the famous Int.Ch. "Garrymhor Faiz-Bu-Hassid".

# CHAPTER II

## EARLY SHOW DOGS

ON the outbreak of the First World War the breeding and exhibiting of Afghans came practically to a complete halt, and no fresh stock was imported of course. In fact it was two years after the war had ended before fresh blood came into Britain in any strength. The first important post-war importers were Major and Mrs. G. Bell Murray, of Kirkpatrick Fleming, Dumfriesshire, Scotland, and their friend Miss Jean C. Manson, of The Cove, at Kirkpatrick Fleming.

## THE BELL MURRAY DOGS

The Bell Murrays and Miss Manson brought at least half a dozen selected dogs and bitches back with them. About these Afghans very few people indeed know anything to-day, but fortunately Miss Clara Bowring, who was one of the leading workers for the breed in its early days, mentioned these very dogs in an article on the Afghan in *Our Dogs*. I will quote a paragraph: ' It was in 1920 that Major and Mrs. Bell Murray accompanied by their friend, Miss Manson, brought back to England the first kennel of Afghans. These consisted of three stud dogs, " Rajah ", a dark fawn with black mask, " Khym " a cream, and " Ooty ", a pale fawn with black mask. The bitches were " Begum ", a cream, " Ranee ", a fawn, " Kanee ", a fawn with black mask and " Pushim ", a golden brindle. Miss Manson had been first attracted to these hounds whilst out riding in Baluchistan, when she met a Sirdar with his hound, " Begum ". Its quaint appearance delighted her but it was only after some time and much bargaining that she induced the Sirdar to sell his dog. Three years after when visiting a native bazaar, " Begum " suddenly recognized her former owner and leapt to greet him with the most touching delight '.

Over the caption ' Major Bell Murray's Trio ' there appears a photograph by the Sport & General Agency of three of these dogs, and a fine head study from the same agents of " Rajah ", in the well-known article by Mrs. O. M. Couper in *Hutchinson's Dog Encyclopædia*, 1935 (pp. 11 and 12 respectively): I have searched the photographer's library for prints of these pictures but regret they are not available, and so I cannot reproduce them here. However, I have managed by an immense amount of hunting to get photographs of other Afghans of about that period.

On Plate III we have a group of four Afghans who were in the possession of Miss D. Evelyn Denyer. Miss Denyer was one of the principal breeders of Afghans in the early 1920's, and although she was the third of the established British breeders (the first two kennels being those of Major and Mrs. Bell Murray and of

Miss Jean C. Manson) she was, I think, the first to have an affix, this being the suffix ' of Kaf '. Miss Denyer became on marriage Mrs. J. Barton but continued her keen interest in the breed. In May 1930 " Ku Mari of Kaf " served by Ch. " Sirdar of Ghazni " produced " Badshah of Ainsdart " (the breeder being Mrs. J. Morris-Jones) who became an International Champion. And in April 1931, another ' of Kaf ' bitch (the last to produce a Cruft's winner), " Zabana of Kaf ", served by " Omar of Geufron " (a son of Ch. " Sirdar of Ghazni ") produced Ch. " Shah Shuja of Geufron ", bred by Mrs. Eileen Drinkwater.

On Mrs. Barton's departure abroad with her husband the ' of Kaf ' dogs were mainly acquired by Captain T. S. Waterlow Fox, whose kennels bore the suffix ' of Wyke '. When the Afghan Hound Club was formed in 1925 Miss Denyer was its first secretary, Captain Waterlow Fox the president and Miss Clara Bowring the treasurer. Miss Denyer had been the principal force behind the formation of the club, and had enjoyed the unstinted support of Major and Mrs. Bell Murray and Miss Manson, of course, and Mr. Will Hally. Mr. Hally has for years since been the leading breed correspondent for the canine Press, and has contributed much in his notes in *Our Dogs* towards fostering interest in the breed.

On the formation of the Afghan Hound Club its supporters drew up what was to become the official Standard. In November 1925 the Kennel Club granted the breed Championship status. The first Challenge Certificates were awarded at Cruft's Dog Show for 1926, and with Mr. A. Croxton Smith judging the winner of the dog C.C. was Mrs. J. Barton's fawn

" Taj Mahip of Kaf " (91GG), while the bitch C.C. winner was Miss J. C. Manson's cream to khaki " Ranee " (93GG). " Taj Mahip of Kaf " was by the cream dog " Khym " (1462GG) out of " Dargai " (94GG), and bred by Major G. Bell Murray born 17th April 1924 ; " Ranee " (93GG) was by " Rajah ", a dark fawn with a black mask, out of the cream bitch " Begum ", also bred by Major Bell Murray and born in March 1919. " Ranee's " portrait is reproduced on Plate III.

The dog " Khym " mentioned was by " Baluch " out of " Ranee ", " Baluch " being also the sire of " Shadi ", who became the first bitch Champion—but I travel a little too far ahead. Let us return a moment to " Taj Mahip of Kaf ", the winner of the first dog C.C. An excellent photograph of this dog (by Thomas Fall) accompanies Miss Denyer's contribution to C. C. Sanderson's *Pedigree Dogs*, 1927. He is a nice looking Afghan with very fair coat for a Bell Murray breeding. Certainly he is in better state than " Tulsi ", another of Miss Denyer's Afghans pictured in the same book, and the bitch of hers used by Ash to illustrate his *Dogs and How to Know Them*, 1925.

## THE ' GHAZNI ' DOGS

In the meantime, in 1925, Mrs. Mary Amps brought from the British Legation in Kabul the dog " Sirdar ". He was a rich red dog bred in the royal kennels of King Amanullah of Afghanistan. On returning to Britain from Kabul, where Mrs. Amps' husband was stationed,

Mrs. Amps registered this dog as " Sirdar of Ghazni"
and founded her celebrated ' Ghazni ' kennels. (Ghazni
is a town some 7,000 feet up in the wilds of Afghanistan,
south of Kabul, the present capital—Ghazni was itself
the capital at one time.)  On being exhibited in Britain
" Sirdar of Ghazni " was at once acclaimed the finest
Afghan seen here since " Zardin "; certainly on the
small side but an ideal Afghan in structure, coat and
temperament.  He won his first C.C. at the Kennel
Club show in 1928, and in seven years won eight
C.Cs.

As a stud force " Sirdar of Ghazni " was also outstand-
ingly successful.  He sired three Champion sons and
three Champion daughters:  Ch. " Asri-Havid of
Ghazni ", Int.Ch. " Badshah of Ainsdart " and Ch.
" Ashna of Ghazni " were his best sons; and these
again produced two further Champion dogs and one
Champion bitch.  Of his other sons, " Omar of
Geufron ", " Abdul of Ghazni ", " Ghazni, son of
Sirdar ", " Shahib of Wahsdarb " and " Shah Zeman of
Wahsdarb ", the celebrated " Omar of Geufron " sired
three Champions out of a single litter of five puppies!
But the Hounds are breeding too fast . . . let us see
what else was happening in the Afghan world in
" Sirdar's " time.

When Mrs. Amps brought " Sirdar " from Kabul she
also brought another dog called " Khan of Ghazni ".
This was the warrior Afghan who slew three leopards
in his native mountains; an animal of the stuff that
our finest dogs were bred from.  Think of this when
viewing the power of the Afghan when unleashed—
and read with me a little of ' The Hounds of
Afghanistan " by Juliette de Baïracli-Levy:

' Hear them! the hounds of Afghanistan,
  As they patrol in the light of the stars,
  Guarding the dark rock forts of their masters,
  Baying hate at Sirius through the night hours.

' See them! the hounds of Afghanistan,
  As they bound o'er the purple plateau of Pamir,
  Mysterious unearthly as a rainbow,
  The silken wild-haired hound pack streaming near.'

In this penultimate poem of *The Cypress Wreath*, 1944, the poetess has caught the character of the Afghan Hound and passed it on to us. Mrs. Amps really did bring us warrior Afghans from Kabul!

I never met " Khan " but I can clearly remember " Sirdar " on the several occasions I called on Mrs. Amps when she was living at Bath, which was my home for many years when I left school and started with dogs under the guidance of Major and Mrs. J. G. E. Gallie. Major Gallie was a veterinary surgeon in Gay Street and his wife ran the Bath Dog Bureau there (I see it is now an antique shop): it was through their kindness to me that I became mixed up with dogs for the quarter of a century that has since passed. I had heard of ' the glorious red dog ' up on Charlcombe and made my first pilgrimage purely to see what an Afghan looked like: I am glad I went now, and afterwards, for had I not, and had not Mrs. Amps and " Sirdar " borne with my many questions this book would not have been written.

In 1927 the first Champion in the breed was made. This was the dog " Buckmal " (1461GG), registered and bred by Major G. Bell Murray, born 21st March 1923, a son of " Ooty " out of " Pushum " (both registered). Ch. " Buckmal " is represented on Plate IV.

He was the property of Miss Jean C. Manson, and was a very intelligent dog according to all accounts I have heard.

Two years later, 1929, the first bitch Champion appeared. This was " Shadi " (1823 H.H.), registered by Miss Manson and bred by Major Bell Murray, born 27th July 1924. A daughter of " Baluch " out of " Oolu ". " Shadi " was transferred to and exhibited by Mrs. A. B. Willans, then of Duchy Avenue, Bradford, and after winning C.Cs. at the Scottish Kennel Club's show, 1927, and at the Royal Veterinary College show, 1927, she attained her third C.C. at Cruft's in 1929.

## OTHER PIONEER KENNELS

By this time the breed was firmly established and there were many kennels breeding the type upon which the modern Afghan has rightly been built. This was in effect a blending of the blood lines of the ' Ghazni ' and the older Bell Murray stock, the result having the good shoulders, height and tails of the latter with the character and coat of the ' Ghazni ' dogs, thus getting the breed much nearer the original " Zardin " ideal. The leading kennels at about this time were the ' Garrymhor ' of Mrs. Olive M. Couper, the ' Wahsdarb ' of Mrs. Isabel Bradshaw, the ' Ainsdart ' of Mrs. Morris-Jones, the ' Kuranda ' of Mrs. B. Rothwell-Fielding, the ' Geufron ' of Mrs. E. Eileen Drinkwater, the ' Baberbagh ' of Mrs. L. Prude, the ' Pushtikuh ' of Miss H. Semple, the ' el Kabul ' of Dr. Betsy Porter, the ' of Chaman ' of Mrs. Molly Sharpe, the ' Tuclo ' of Mrs. Sydney Rhodes, the ' Westmill ' of Mrs. M.

Wood, and the kennels of Mrs. J. Chesterfield-Cooke,
and of Mrs. M. E. Till. These were the dozen or so
of the principal kennels of the period between the
arrival of the ' Ghazni ' dogs and the Second World
War ; one or two are still breeding to-day.

Let us briefly see who they were. Mrs. Couper's
kennel was a quite early one, based on ' Ghazni ' blood.
The first two Afghans Mrs. Couper had were " Kym of
Wyke " and " Sheba of Wyke ", a brace bred in Captain
Waterlow Fox's kennels (typical Bell Murray dogs), but
on seeing " Sirdar of Ghazni " she decided to build her
kennels on stock bred from him. I think " Omar of
Geufron " and " Riverleigh Sirdar " (sons of " Sirdar ")
helped Mrs. Couper most in founding the ' Garrymhor '
kennel which later became so well known. Incidentally, the blood blending of " Omar " and " Sheba "
produced Ch. " Malati of Geufron " . . . more evidence
even then that a union of the heavy-coated and light-
coated strains was desirable. The ' Wahsdarb ' affix
was, of course, Mrs. Bradshaw's surname spelt backwards (a device which although generally rather ugly
and cumbersome, gave in this particular case almost an
Eastern flavour). The ' Ainsdart ' kennel of Mrs.
Morris-Jones produced an International Champion,
" Badshah of Ainsdart ", by " Sirdar of Ghazni " out of
" Ku Mari of Kaf ", bred in May 1930 ; he was bought
by Mrs. M. Wood, got his third C.C. at the Ladies'
Kennel Association show in 1933 and then went to the
U.S.A.

Mrs. Rothwell-Fielding and Mrs. Drinkwater no
longer keep kennels but during the Twenty Years
Peace they were both keen breeders. Mrs. Rothwell-
Fielding is still a keen student of the Afghan and in

the past bravely pursued questions of vital importance to the breed. Mrs. Drinkwater bred at her ' Geufron ' kennels (principally when she was at West Kirby) more Champions than have been bred at any other kennels. When I wrote an article on the Afghan for *The Tail-Wagger Magazine* (published January 1937) I had some interesting letters from Mrs. Drinkwater accompanied with photographs of some of her dogs. On Plate V I reproduce two of these, one showing Ch. " Agha Lala of Geufron " sitting with Mrs. Drinkwater.

West Kirby seems to have a soft spot for Afghans for Dr. Betsy Porter also established her ' el Kabul ' kennels there, in Caldy Road. At least one of Dr. Porter's Afghans was a son of " Zabana of Kaf ", thus still carrying the oldest of Afghan affixes, this dog being her Ch. " Shah Shuja of Geufron " bred by Mrs. Drinkwater in April 1931, his sire being " Omar of Geufron " (the clever Hound often referred to since as ' The Old Bard of West Kirby '). On Plate VII we have a picture of " Marika of Baberbagh ", one of Mrs. Prude's Afghans, and it is interesting to note that the dog on the left of the illustration in Plate V of three dogs owned by Mrs. G. E. W. Jüngeling, Ch. " Baber of Baberbagh ", became a Sieger in 1932.

Mrs. Molly Sharpe, the well-known breed correspondent to the dog papers, owned one of the most famous of Afghans, Int-Ch. " Garrymhor Faiz-Bu-Hassid " (see Plate XIV), a fine dog bred by Mrs. Couper to become Mrs. Sharpe's first Afghan. He sired several Champions three of whom were the American Ch. " Juan of Chaman ", the Canadian Ch. " Pic of Chaman " and the Italian Ch. " Sabue of Chaman ". This dog was still winning at the age of eleven years in veteran classes at Championship shows, and died at the age of thirteen in 1948. In 1938 another Champion of Mrs. Sharpe's, Ch. " Taj Akbar of Chaman ", was televised from Alexandra Palace, probably being the first Afghan to appear in television. This famous dog set up a record for the breed by winning nine C.Cs. at the age of three years. Mrs. Sharpe's dogs took both the C.Cs. offered at the first post-war show offering them to Afghans; " Taj of Chaman " (son of Ch. " Taj Akbar ") winning the dog C.C. and " Tajavia of Chaman " the bitch C.C., being awarded them by Brig-General L. F. F. Lance. " Taj " is now an International Champion and " Tajavia " a Champion: in fact Int.Ch. " Taj of Chaman " holds an extremely fine record for he has never been beaten by any other Afghan . ; . as far as I can trace the early " Zardin " and the modern " Taj " are the only British Afghans to have been unbeaten in their breed.

Mrs. Wood's ' Westmill ' kennels has contributed tremendously to the healthy development of the breed. Her Ch. " Westmill Ben Havid " attained his title in 1934, as did another ' Westmill ' dog, Ch. " Tamasar ". Ch. " Westmill Karabagh " (born 1933—died 1946) took her title in 1935, being the property of Mrs. Sydney Rhodes. Mrs. Rhodes has been in Afghans for twenty years and her ' Tuclo ' kennel is known all over the world. Her early Champions included " Karabagh ", " Bethsheba " and " Westmill Charbara ", while post-war Champions are the two bitches " Ajawaan Chita Mia " and " Ajawaan Rani Tamba ".

Of the smaller and in many cases later pre-war kennels we have not space to give more than a brief run over. These were Miss A. M. M. Simmons' ' Bericote ' kennels, Mrs. Casson's 'Khan' kennels, the 'Brant-wood' owned by Mr. H. A. Hill and Miss L. S. Moss, the 'Enriallic' Irish kennel of Mr. Daniel I. Cronin, Mrs. Cooper's 'De Flandre', Miss M. C. Mathews' 'Westover' kennels (where Afghan wool is still spun and knitted into women's wear!), Mrs. D. Clarke's 'of Valdorern' and Miss M. C. C. Clarke's 'of Kandahar' kennels, the 'Jalalabad' of Miss F. G. Ide, and the 'Turkuman' kennel where Miss Juliette de Baïracli-Levy has reared many fine dogs on natural methods.

The 'Enriallic' Afghans bred the first International Champion in the breed. This was the bitch "Zandi of Enriallic", by "Rupee" (17,555) out of "Souriya" (17,556), born 26th December 1932, and who attained her Irish and British titles in 1935. She was the property of Mr. Daniel I. Cronin of Killarney. I published a fine head study of this bitch in my article on the breed in *The Tail-Wagger Magazine*, January 1937. Incidentally, the first Afghan to be registered with the Irish Kennel Club was Lt.-Col. W. Adye-Curran's (of Blackrock, Co. Dublin) "Kibi of Cove" (8206), registered 22nd April 1927. "Kibi" was bred by Miss Jean C. Manson (the Miss Manson whom we have already met) and was born 19th October 1926, sire "Potentate", dam "Aru". Another even more famous Afghan of about the time of "Zandi" was Mrs. A. Bhanubandh's Int.Ch. "Chota Sahib". He took his qualifying C.C. at the Scottish Kennel Club show in 1936 and also became an Irish Champion.

But a still more celebrated dog was Ch. "Asri-Havid of Ghazni", to whom I briefly alluded earlier. 'Rif', as was his nickname, was the first Afghan to be awarded

Plate V

Mrs. Mary Amps, who founded the
' Ghazni ' kennels in 1925.

*Photo by Stuart Black*

Mrs. E. E. Drinkwater
with Ch.
" Agha Lala of Geufron "
and
" Aswakarna of Geufron ".

Mrs. G. E. W.
Jüngeling's " Baber
of Baberbagh ",
" Nadir of Ghazni "
and
" Shahib of
Wahsdarb ".

*Photo by Het Leven.*

Plate VI

Mrs. Phyllis Robson with her
famous Ch.
" Asri-Havid of Ghazni ".

*Courtesy Mrs. Robson.*

Mrs. Molly Sharpe's Ch.
" Taj Akbar of Chaman ".

*Photo by Scottish Pictorial Press.*

Mrs. Molly Sharpe's
" Garrymhor
Faiz-Bu-Hassid ".

*Photo by Fall.*

the Best in Show prize, and was also the first black-and-tan Champion Afghan in the world.   A son of Ch. "Sirdar of Ghazni" he was bred by Mrs. Mary Amps and became the sire himself of Ch. "Westmill Ben Havid", and other outstanding dogs.   He was Mrs. Phyllis Robson's one and only Afghan and devoted friend of some ten years ;   he took ill from duodenal ulcers in May 1937 and died after a severe hæmorrhage the following month (24th June 1937). Ch. "Asri-Havid of Ghazni" had a most beautiful head and expression, and he passed this on (with his excellent gait) to his progeny.   Mr. F. T. Daws painted his portrait, and this was reproduced in the *Dog World,* 2nd July 1937.   On Plate VI we see him sitting with Mrs. Robson in a portrait taken many years ago.

Mrs. Robson having had but a single Afghan and yet that dog having become so well known reminds me of how an Afghan I knew very well indeed attracted perhaps as much attention in the theatre world as did "Lassie" in the film world.   This dog was "Kym", who played in the film 'Lorna Doone' in the palace scene, and in some other films, but who appeared principally in the many plays running in the Shaftesbury Avenue precincts during 1935 and 1936.   I think his longest run was throughout the whole of the duration of the play 'Theatre Royal', held at the Lyric with Dame Marie Tempest, Madge Titheradge and Margaret Vines in the cast.   "Kym" worked every evening without fail, and matinées too, for I think he was five months in that play, and knew the sniff of every piece of property on the stage.   He was owned by Mrs. Rhoda E. Flanders who ran the Moorvale Dog Depot in Rupert Street, and who in between breeding

Pekingese used to hire out trained dogs to film companies and theatres . . . at least he was owned by her as much as he would let anyone at all own him, for he had ideas of attachment to whomever he liked. I was about that time running a dog shop in Richmond for Mrs. Flanders and, of course, knew " Kym " extremely well. He would please himself whether he would have a bed and breakfast with me at my digs in Victoria or stay and guard the Rupert Street shop . . . given half a chance he would trot off with Margaret Vines. The last time I saw him was when Mrs. Flanders, " Kym " and I went down to Bristol to the Ideal Homes Exhibition, at the Colston Hall there, with Pekes and Persians all on a stand, and the loyal old dog collected money for the Bristol Dogs' Home.

# CHAPTER III

## CONTEMPORARY DOGS

SINCE the end of the Second World War at least a score of people have taken up breeding Afghan Hounds, some of whom had for many years bred other breeds. With half a dozen years' experience of Afghan breeding most of these breeders are better able to visualize the ideal Afghan and get that little nearer to it that makes all the hard work of breeding so well worth while. The result is that the set-back the futile years of war cost us has been to a very large extent eradicated in this breed, and one or two of the present-day Afghans would be quite capable of holding their own against a representative selection of pre-war dogs.

One of the first modern dogs who comes to mind as an outstanding post-war success is Ch. " Ravelly Patrols Ali Bey ", owned by Mr. Reg A. Floyd of the ' Ravelly ' kennels of Afghans and Wire-haired Fox Terriers. " Ali Bey " was bred by Mrs. Ruth Y. Harrison (' Patrols ') by " Turkuman Dammar Pine Tree " out of " Patrols Creme Chenille ", and has been handled by Mr. H. A. Southgate. At the time of writing I hear he has won twelve Challenge Certificates, has been Best in Show no less than seventy times, and has won over 300 first prizes, which makes a remarkable record. His sire, "Turkuman Dammar Pine Tree", was bred by Miss Doris Venn of the 'Conygar' affix and is now ten years old. Though "Ali Bey" is his most celebrated son he has been consistently siring winners right from the end of the war ; he has been sire or grandsire of some 30—40 per cent of the winners at very many of the big shows. He is, of course, the property of Miss M. C. Mathews ('Westover'), who bought him from Miss de Baïracli-Levy. What is most important about "Ali Bey", however, is that he became the first post-war Champion dog, qualifying under Mrs. S. Rhodes at Altrincham, September 1947.

The sire and dam of "Ravelly Patrols Ali Bey" produced in a later litter another fine dog, Ch. "Patrols Ali Khan", who has brought additional credit to his breeder, Mrs. Ruth Y. Harrison. Small wonder Cheshire folk have often referred to Afghans as 'West Kirby Hounds', for many of the most typical specimens have been produced there, by Mrs. Drinkwater at 'Geufron', by Dr. Betsy Porter in Caldy Road, and now by Mrs. Harrison in Broxton Avenue!

The first post-war Champion bitch was Mrs. Sydney Rhodes' "Ajawaan Chita Mia". With Ch. "Ajawaan Rani Tamba" in her 'Tuclo' kennels as well Mrs. Rhodes has two post-war Champion bitches ; this is the only kennel to have two (they were both bred by Mrs. King, of Liverpool, out of "Silvercaul Sa de Miranda"). Mrs. Rhodes bred three Champions before the war, as I have said in the previous chapter.

Miss Eileen Snelling of the 'Khorrassan' kennel at Bickenhill, Caversham, has been an extraordinarily active and successful exhibitor and breeder. She owns a variety of colours including pure whites and blacks with chinchilla markings, the latter a most attractive shade, and has been very busy exporting Afghan youngsters far and wide. On Plate VIII we see a typical ' Khorrassan ' quartet. Also at Caversham is the smaller kennel of ' Palitana ' Afghans owned by Miss Patricia Burchett.

The ' Netheroyd ' kennels belong to Mr. and Mrs. E. Abson of Huddersfield, who have bred some really fine dogs. On Plate XI we see two of their dogs, " Netheroyd Ansari " and the young bitch " Netheroyd Chaya " who has won two C.Cs. Her dam, Ch. " Netheroyd Turkuman Camelthorn " served by " Ansari " produced Ch. " Netheroyd Alibaba " in November 1947, and this dog won the Best of Breed at Cruft's 1950 (his photograph is reproduced on Plate X). " Netheroyd Turkuman Camelthorn " was I am almost certain, the first black Champion bitch. She was formerly the property of Miss Juliette de Baïracli-Levy (' Turkuman ') having been given to her by Mrs. Clarke who had her as her pick of a litter from Mrs. J. V. Polson's " Golden Ranee " in lieu of a stud service by " Turkuman Pomegranate ". This fine bitch won six C.Cs. in 1948 and has since been retired from show. Before transfer this bitch was " Turkuman Camelthorn " and served by " Chota Nissim of Ringbank " she produced the magnificent Afghan exported to and now leading the way in America, Ch. " Turkuman Nissim's Laurel ".

So far I have had occasion to refer in this chapter to Mr. Reg. Floyd's ' Ravelly ' kennels, to Mrs. Ruth Y. Harrison (' Patrols '), Mr. and Mrs. Edgar Abson (' Netheroyd '), Mrs. Sydney Rhodes (' Tuclo '), Miss

Eileen Snelling ('Khorrassan'), and Miss Doris Venn ('Conygar'). There are others of course but it is impossible to more than briefly list those who come to mind as I think of the leading post-war breeders in the British Isles. Mrs. F. C. Riley of Birchington owns the 'Bletchingley' kennels where her "Bletchingley Tajomeer" is the stud force; his most celebrated daughter is surely Ch. "Bletchingley Zara", who won Best of Breed at Cruft's 1948 and holds five C.Cs. The Baroness Westenholz ('Closmidi') combines in her kennel the substantial blood lines of 'Kuranda' and 'Chaman' and has bred some really nice stock, including the upstanding red dog (of twenty-nine inches!) "Rashnee of Closmidi", owned by Mr. Bellerby and Mrs. Cooper. "Rashnee's" sire was "Conygar Baradar", and his dam "Juanita of Chaman"; he is six years old now and reminds many of us of old "Sirdar of Ghazni".

Other names are Mrs. D. Hall of Preston, who at her 'Barbille' establishment breeds Afghans, Miniature Poodles, Chow Chows and Siamese cats. Mrs. Hall is very well known to show-goers, of course, for she generally has a prominent stand for the sale of the best dog books at all Championship shows. What Mrs. Casson has done in introducing the Afghan to North Wales Mrs. Betti Sullivan is now doing with her kennels at Aberfan in South Wales. Mrs. C. A. Jenkins of Folkestone, has returned to her favourite breed and I see that among other old friends Miss Mathews ('Westover') and Mrs. J. V. Polson of the 'Khassar' kennel are still busy in the breed. Also working to further the interests of the Afghan Hound are Miss Joanne Chambers ('Otontala'), Mrs. F. W. Cockings

('Murgar'), Mrs. S. Devitt ('of Carloway'), Miss J. L. Edwards ('of Satania'), Mrs. J. H. Parker ('of Three Streams'), Mrs. Kara Tziros ('of Tzaharane'), Mrs. M. Scarff and Miss J. R. Scarff, and Mrs. Z. M. S. Muir and Mr. S. J. Fernley Jones who together run the 'Densevarg' kennel at Gravesend.

In Ireland Mrs. M. O'Toole's 'Kohistan' kennel has contributed substantially to Afghan progress. Her Ch. "Vendas Tash-Down" at the age of twelve years entered Cruft's show of 1948 and won the dog C.C. and the Hound group classes, thus becoming an International Champion, even at that age. His appearance and success caused some surprise to newcomers to the breed and helped to generally remind us that some of the pre-war stalwarts have kept remarkably fit.

A little further across dividing waters we must not forget the fine stock being bred in the Channel Isles by Mrs. Howard Gibson at her 'Acklam' kennels, Jersey. One of her best dogs is Ch. "Mohammed Ali of Acklam", who won his third C.C. at Chester under Mrs. Sydney Rhodes. "Mohammed Ali" was bred by Mrs. Gibson by "Turkuman Dammar Pine Tree" out of Ch. "Mitzou of Acklam", and is a litter brother of "Amanullah Khan of Acklam" now in Belgium and the property of Mme. Mariette Deckers.

## EUROPEAN KENNELS

On the European mainland there are many supporters of the Afghan Hound and kennels are becoming established in most countries of Western Europe and Scandinavia. Mme. Mariette Deckers, the international judge, has a growing kennel at Antwerp,

Belgium, and her black-and-tan " Amanullah Khan of Acklam " (Plate XI) has won the supreme honours at French and Belgian Championship shows. Mme. Deckers bred from this dog a fine litter out of her Int.Ch. " Suki of Chaman " in the spring of 1950. Also well known are the ' Kaboul ' kennels of M. J. A. Appels in Belgium (M. Appels is the president of the Belgian Afghan Hound club), the ' Oranje Menage ' kennels of Miss Eva Pauptit and those of Mrs. M. Wilson in the Netherlands, and the kennels of Fr. Stockmann in Switzerland.

In Scandinavia Afghans are spreading throughout all three countries principally by export (and re-export) from the leading kennels in Norway, the ' Khasru ', owned by Sigurd Bruun Tønnessen and Isabella Cavallini Tønnessen of Oslo. On Plate IX I have included illustrations of some of their best dogs. The Tønnessens breed on a large scale and exhibit widely. At the first post-war international show held in Norway (in 1946) sixteen of their Afghans were entered by them ; and their team has collected numerous supreme awards in Norway and Sweden. In the illustration of six Afghans side by side there is one International Champion (" Kuranda ") and one Norwegian Champion (" Knamba "). Their foundation bitch, Int-Ch. " Khasru ", was from Mrs. Sharpe's kennels, and it is after this twelve-year-old bitch that the kennel gets its name.

## AMERICAN KENNELS

Before concluding this rather brief survey of contemporary Afghan kennels let us see what is the posi-

Plate VII

Mrs. Marion Florsheim
with Int.Ch.
" Rudiki of Prides Hill ".

*Photo by Van Dam.*

Mrs. L. Prude's
" Marika
of Baberbagh ".

*Photo by Robinson.*

Mrs. Molly Sharpe's
Int.Ch.
" Taj of Chaman ".

*Photo by Rushbrook, Edinburgh.*

Plate VIII

Miss Eileen Snelling with
" Portrait ", " Ivory ",
" Peridot " and " Marabout ",
all ' of Khorrassan '.

[*Photo by*      [*Sussex Daily News*

Six dogs from Mrs. Mary Matchett's Canadian kennels, Int.Ch. " Kurram ", and Ch
" Saranga ", " Khyber ", " Hindukist ", " Tükh " and " Rahman ", all ' El Myia

Plate IX

Sigurd Bruun Tønnessen with
Nor.Ch. " Knamba ",
" Kalah ", " Kibaba " and
" Khamoora ".

Six dogs from Mrs. Tønnessen's Norwegian kennels, Int.Ch. " Kuranda ", Nor.Ch.
" Knamba ", " Khamoora ", " Kibaba ", " Kalah " and " Kinzuka ".

Plate X

Int.Ch. " Rudiki of Prides Hill ", after a painting by Edwin Megargee.

Mr. Edgar Abson's Ch. " Netheroyd Alibaba ".

*Photo by Fox Photos Ltd.*

Two Int.Chs. " Rana of Chaman " and " Rudiki of Prides Hill ", by Megargee.

tion in America. It is simple enough to pick on a starting point for running over American Afghans, however short an allusion space may allow, for if there was ever one outstanding dog over there it was Int.Ch. "Rudiki of Prides Hill". This magnificent dog was born 8th August 1937, a son of the famous Int.Ch. "Badshah of Ainsdart" (whose name appears in practically every pedigree of importance in the U.S.A.), a son of the great Ch. "Sirdar of Ghazni". As "Rudiki" matured he was recognized as being almost an exact copy of his grandsire, "Sirdar" (in coat he was even richer). He belonged to Mrs. Marion Foster Florsheim of the 'Five Miles' kennels, and the two were practically inseparable companions for the ten years of his life. As a show exhibit "Rudiki" was a phenomenal success: fifteen times he was Best in Show, twenty-seven times Best American-bred in Show, forty-four times Best Hound, seventy-three placed in group, and seventy-seven the best Afghan! But that was not the be-all and end-all of his existence by a long chalk, for he proved himself a most potent stud force and sired over 200 puppies carrying the finest blood in America. He died on Christmas Eve, 1947.

Mrs. Florsheim started her kennels about the time of the outbreak of the Second World War, and although she was away for a while serving as a pilot in the American army she ran things so well that by the time the kennels were closed after the death of "Rudiki" some 300—400 fine puppies had been bred at 'Five Miles'. Another famous Afghan of Mrs. Florsheim (later in the ownership of Miss Margaret Hawkins) was Int.Ch. "Rana of Chaman", exported by Mr. Reg. Floyd (after winning ninety firsts in Britain) and bred

by Mrs. M. Sharpe. "Rana" developed a malignant
growth in the neck and had to be painlessly destroyed
in the beginning of July 1949.

Another great dog who died in the meantime was
Mrs. Olive Couper's "Garrymhor Rudari", who was
about the last of the bitches directly carrying the blood
of "Sirdar". She died in September 1948 aged
thirteen. Her brother became American Ch.
"Garrymhor Zabardast of Arken".

While it is true that some of the great ones have
passed on and left gaps in the ranks of the Afghan
fancy at home and abroad it is most gratifying to find
that the promising youngsters of a few years back are
turning out genuine flyers. One such dog who has fulfilled every hope of his breeder and owner is Ch. "Turkuman Nissim's Laurel", a really fine dog now
approaching his prime and winning at every event
where shown. He was bred by Mr. Edgar Abson
('Netheroyd') by "Chota Nissim of Ringbank" out
of "Turkuman Camelthorn", and was Miss Juliette
de Baïracli-Levy's breeding-term selection from the
dam's first litter; he was then reared according to the
natural method advocated by Miss de Baïracli-Levy,
making the fifth generation of a naturally reared
'Turkuman' strain.

Like his dam he is black and with white markings,
these being a blaze, a bib and neat front socks: black
Afghans are a feature of the 'Turkuman' strain, certainly as far back as "Nissim's Laurel's" great-grand-
sire, a huge black Hound who used to sit on the door-
step of 37 Talbot Road, W.2, like a figurehead when
Miss de Baïracli-Levy was a neighbour of mine . . . it
is probably from that giant that "Nissim's Laurel"

has inherited the beard I think so well befits an Afghan. However, American Ch. "Turkuman Nissim's Laurel" is now the joint property of Mr. Sol Malkin (the American writer) and Mrs. Evan Shay, and won his required number of points in 1947. To-day he is still winning: his record for 1950 being Best in Show at the Afghan Hound speciality show, Best of Breed at the great Westminster Kennel Club show, Best Hound (same show), and Best of Breed at the Chicago International show . . . which is really something to write home about.

But, of course, there are many Champions and International Champions in the U.S.A. for although the Afghan only 'caught on' in the 1930's the number of breeders there now is surprisingly high. The Afghan Hound Club of America was formed about 1935, and due to the pioneer work of Mr. Shaw McKeen, Mrs. Robert F. Bodger, Miss A. White, the late Mrs. W. E. Porter (' Kingsway '), Mrs. Madelaine Austin, Mrs. D. A. Holmes, Mrs. A. B. Dewitt, Mr. Charles A. Wernsman, and Dr. Eugene Beck the Club grew until to-day it is the parent club for the breed in America. Since its official recognition in 1938 the A.H.C.A. has had the following presidents: Mrs. Sherman R. Hoyt, the late Mrs. Jack Oakie (of the ' Oakvardon' kennels, whose Ch. "Barberry Hill Dolly" was extremely popular), Mr. Charles A. Wernsman (a founder member), Mrs. Robert F. Bodger (the original secretary), and Mrs. E. F. McConaha. Mrs. Bodger and Miss Charlotte Coffey have shared the secretaryship throughout the life of the Club.

I cannot possibly list all the leading kennels in the U.S.A. but as British breeders are interested in

American pedigrees and affixes I think the following should certainly be mentioned: primarily, of course, the 'Five Miles' establishment of Mrs. Marion Foster Florsheim of New York, then the 'Grandeur' kennels of Mrs. Evans ('Sunny') Shay in Connecticut, the 'Arken' kennels of Mr. Charles A. Wernsman (mentioned earlier) and the 'Windtryst' owned by Mrs. Ward Monroe French in Pennsylvania (whose charming picture appears on Plate XVI). Miss Kay Finch of California (who has done for the Afghan in sculpture what Edwin Megargee and F. T. Daws have in their paintings) owns the 'Crown Crest' kennels, Mrs. Lauer J. Froelich of Indiana the 'of Elcoza' kennels, Mr. and Mrs. Herbert A. Brothers of Ohio the 'Arthea', and Miss A. White of New Mexico the 'Kandahar'. Mrs. Sherman R. Hoyt, who is, of course, very well known over here as a judge and breeder of Poodles, raises Afghans at her 'Blakeen' establishment in Connecticut, Mr. and Mrs. Lemuel Ayers run the 'Balmor' kennels in New York, Mr. and Mrs. Frederick A. Jagger of New Jersey own the 'Majara' kennels and in Pennsylvania Dr. William H. Ivens has his 'Holiday House' kennels.

In Canada undoubtedly the kennels we hear most about are those owned by Mrs. Mary Matchett and those of Mrs. Eva Gudgeon. Mrs. Matchett's kennels are the 'El Myia' at Ontario, where numerous Champions have been bred and owned: six of the 'El Myia' dogs appear on Plate VIII. The 'Birchwood' kennels of Mrs. Gudgeon are also in Ontario.

# CHAPTER IV

**Characteristics**—The Afghan Hound should be dignified and aloof with a certain keen fierceness. The Eastern or Oriental expression is typical of the breed. The Afghan looks at and through one.

**General Appearance**—The gait of the Afghan Hound should be smooth and springy with a style of high order. The whole appearance of the dog should give the impression of strength and dignity combining speed and power. The head must be held proudly.

**Head and Skull**—Skull long, not too narrow, with prominent occiput. Foreface long with punishing jaws and slight stop. The skull well balanced and surmounted by a long topknot. Nose preferably black but liver is no fault in light-coloured dogs.

**Eyes**—Should be dark but golden colour is not debarred. Nearly triangular, slanting slightly upwards from the inner corner to the outer.

**Ears**—Set low and well back, carried close to the head. Covered with long silky hair.

49

**Mouth**—Level.

**Neck**—Long and strong with proud carriage of the head.

**Forequarters**—Shoulders long and sloping, well set back, well muscled and strong without being loaded. Forelegs straight and well boned, straight with shoulders, elbows held in.

**Body**—Back level, of moderate length, well muscled and falling slightly away to the tail. Loins straight, broad and rather short. A fair spring of ribs and good depth of chest.

**Hindquarters**—Powerful, with well bent and well turned stifles. Hip-bones rather prominent and wide apart. Great length between hips and hocks with a comparatively short distance between hocks and feet. The dew-claws may be removed or allowed to remain, at the discretion of the breeder.

**Feet**—Forefeet strong and very large both in length and breadth, and covered with long thick hair, toes arched. Pasterns long and springy, especially in front, and the pads well down on the ground. Hind feet long, but not quite so broad as forefeet, and covered with long thick hair.

**Tail**—Not too short. Set on low with a ring at the end. Raised in action. Sparsely feathered.

**Coat**—Long and very fine texture on ribs, fore- and hindquarters and flanks. From the shoulders backwards and along the saddle the hair should be short and close in mature dogs. Hair long from the forehead backward on the head, with a distinct silky topknot; on the foreface the hair is short, as on the back. Ears and legs well coated. Pasterns

can be bare. Coat must be allowed to develop
naturally.

**Colour**—All colours are acceptable.

**Weight and Size**—Ideal height: Dogs 27—29 inches.
Bitches 2—3 inches smaller.

**Faults**—Any appearance of coarseness. Skull too wide
and foreface too short. Weak underjaw. Large
round or full eyes. Neck should never be too
short or thick. Back too long or too short.

## Some Further Notes

There then we have the official Standard of desired
points as drawn up many years ago and revised by
about a dozen of our best breeders in 1946, and still
further adapted slightly by the Kennel Club (Standards
Committee). What alterations I have made are merely
minor literals which I think help to clarify still further.
A Standard has to be completely free of verbiage and
pomposities, of pseudo-anatomical terms and general
obscurities, and (as I said in *The Dachshund Handbook*, 1950, where I had to work pretty hard on the
not-very-plain Standards of Dachshunde) it should be
as simple as pip. Clarity should come above all else, I
think. Compared with other Standards that for the
Afghan is indeed quite well drawn up and easy to
follow, although I think it could stand a little added
information without being overburdened.

'Mouth—Level' does not tell us a great deal: it
would not hurt to add, say, that the teeth should be
large and sound, closing with a scissor-like action so

that when shut the lower incisors are just behind but in contact with the upper incisors. The old hands in the breed know this but novices (especially those who may have come to the Afghan from a different type of breed) will possibly be glad to have detailed information on each point in the Standard.

The Faults paragraph could be enlarged a trifle I think, to include bad shoulders, straight hindquarters, cringing character, poor gait, very light eyes, a stiff poker tail and poor head carriage.

Apart from the addition of these few items I believe the Afghan Standard one of the best I have had to deal with. I do think novices should note with particular attention a few special points in this Standard. In the Characteristics paragraph the words 'dignified and aloof with a certain keen fierceness' occur: these really portray the true Afghan character and temperament, and no Afghan worth his breeding should lack them; the Afghan is rather demonstrative, and at times a little turbulent, and this is exactly as he should be.

In the next paragraph we find he should be 'smooth and springy' in gait: this is, I think, a most important characteristic of the breed and a good gait should always be aimed at. And in dealing with the neck the Standard tells us the head should be proudly carried by it: this also is an important feature, for without the well-raised head the springy and good stepping action cannot be fulfilled.

Finally about the coat: the saddle hair should be *naturally* short and close; the topknot really distinct as the Standard requires; and bare pasterns allowed (bearing in mind the natural interpretation of the Standard that although knees 'can be' bare, fully

Plate XI

Mme. M. Deckers'
Belgian winner
" Amanullah Khan
of Acklam ".

*Photo by Dim.*

The black Champion
bitch " Netheroyd
Turkuman
Camelthorn ".

Mr. Edgar Abson's
" Netheroyd Ansari "
and
" Netheroyd Chaya "

*Photo by
Atkinson, Huddersfield.*

Plate XII

Mme. Mariette Deckers with her
" Amanullah Khan of Acklam ".

*Photo by Dim.*

Mrs. Molly Sharpe's
pre-war team of
racing Afghans.

*Photo by*
*Scottish Pictorial Press*

Mrs. F. C. Riley's Ch.
" Bletchingley Zara ".

*Photo by Sims.*

dressed legs are preferred. Beards are not mentioned
in the Standard but they appeared in many of the old
Afghans and are very attractive . . . I like them,
especially those worn by some of the 'Westmill' and
'Turkuman' Afghans, but of course they do not commonly occur. However, I raise the point as novices may
just happen to find a beard or two developing on their
dogs and in consulting the Standard wonder what to do
about them: on the whole I think most of us like
them when they do appear.

Colours are numerous, and the Standard is generous
in allowing all. The one fact we must remember is
that there is no best colour and that judges do not consider (or should not consider) colour when judging,
except for noting its tone and quality. Before the
Second World War reds and fawns generally led the
way, although chinchillas and creams occasionally came
along. To-day we have pure whites, pure blacks, black-
and-tans, reds, tricolours, silver blues and brindles, as
well as the other colours.

Miss Eileen Snelling appears to easily lead the way
with whites, and has done for some years. Mrs. Eileen
Drinkwater too had whites in the old days, and I
should expect to find most of the British-bred whites
have descended from her old brood bitch " Sita of
Geufron", the dam of Int.Ch. " Amra Singh of
Geufron " who went to Switzerland to further the
attraction to whites on the Continent.

# CHAPTER V

## BREEDING

The parents represent the foundation stock of a kennel, and as you can only breed out of them whatever is in themselves and their ancestors it is obvious then why they should be the best you can afford. The novice with quite a bit of money to spend can buy both a good dog and a good bitch, while the man with little money had better concentrate on getting a good youngish bitch and having her served by a suitable stud, thus saving the difference between the stud's fee and his actual value.

## SIRE AND DAM

If the novice cannot persuade an expert on the variety he wishes to take up to choose his bitch for him then he can at least do the next best thing by swotting up the Standard until *all* the important points are memorized, and he is capable of visualizing those points in the living dog, and then judge which bitch will best suit his kennels and his purse. This is easier said than

done—very much easier. I doubt if every judge of
Afghans is capable of reciting the Standard from
memory . . . it would not hurt to have all judges do so
before ' passing-out ' (as a judge, I mean, not collapsing
with the effort). So let the new breeder swot his
Standard, visualize his perfect bitch, and then go search
for her. He will probably find her after visiting many
big shows and more kennels, but in time he will appre-
ciate that she will be not quite what he thought she
was—experienced breeders do not always sell their very
best to potential competitors although for the most part
they like to put a fellow on the right track in order to
encourage him to the breed. Therefore this first choice
should be made without indecent haste.

Make a thorough examination, and begin at the
beginning: check the head for proportions and shape
of skull, colour and placement and size of eyes, ear sets
and length, jaws, dentition and lips ; check the body
for symmetry and knit, levelness of top-line, depth of
chest, spring of rib, couplings, quarters, legs for
strength and bone, feet and tail ; the coat for texture,
density and health ; colour for correctness and positioning ; action both in the walk and trot ; the mental
reaction, nerves and alertness . . . and don't forget to
look for a sparkle in the eyes and a wag of the tail.

If you find all this a simple matter then you are
doing well indeed: what is harder still is the study of
the bitch's pedigree . . . for remember that the pedigree
must be as good-looking as the bitch herself. There is
little point in your having parent stock of the ideal
type if they cannot produce likenesses of themselves.
Thus when having got your potential brood bitch have
her served by a suitable stud. He may be perfect in all

respects but is more likely to be one not necessarily even a Champion but possessing a very good reputation for siring winners, or very good youngsters at any rate. If your bitch is weak in any one point then do make sure the stud used is perfect in that particular point. Let us say, for example, the bitch has eyes which are much too large: the stud should then be perfect or near perfect in eyes, and not small in eyes, though better small than large, of course. Weakness is counteracted by strength as we all know, but in dog breeding you should not go to the opposite extreme and use a dog with small eyes, for if you do you will find your litter will have say two large-eyed and two small-eyed pups (with no correct-eyed pups in the litter), while by using a stud with perfect eyes you could confidently expect at least some pups with correct eyes. And the same goes for the pedigree of the bitch you begin with, of course, for it should show that right way back her ancestors were good matrons, were neither lean nor too fleshy, were temperamentally steady yet with ample dog-sense and initiative . . . a bitch with such history and character should make a good dam indeed.

In most breeds it is advisable to let the young bitch pass her first season without mating and so begin breeding at the second season, and this is really better too for the Afghan. However, this breed is rather slow in sexual development and if the first season does not come along until she is a year old (occasionally a bitch may be older still) then a bitch can be mated at her first season without harm, depending on her condition and temperament. Again it is generally a good plan to rest a bitch alternate seasons, but with an Afghan she could manage nicely with a rest at say every third season without being too great a drain on her resources. The Afghan is not at all an insensitive dog, and a maiden bitch may experience shock enough if nervous at the first menstrual flow, without having to prepare the as yet undeveloped mind to the ordeals of mating, gestation, whelping and rearing in succession. Remember Nature's clock can be trusted—it was not mass-produced.

If you can afford to begin with a dog as well as a bitch then by all means have one. The better the breeding behind him the more likely he is to sire good stock from decent bitches; and the better stock he produces the higher the fee you can ask, in time to come. He must be mature before being put to work, however, and it is better if he can have his first sexual experiences with an experienced old lady, for the brood bitches will teach him all the quicker. It may even be harmful to put a young greenhorn to a young, inexperienced and excitable bitch, or a fractious or unwilling older one. And better, too, to be about at the time in case help is needed, though it is true of the Afghan as of any other breed that some studs resent interference of any kind.

## MATING

On the one hand the actual mating may take place as quietly and efficiently as those of street mongrels who at one moment have not yet met and at the next are tied in the middle of the road. Yet, on the other hand, there may be the very dickens of a job getting the stud to serve his bitch correctly. A lot of trouble comes about by bringing a bitch to a dog too early or too late in season, but there may be other reasons as well. Courtship helps tremendously, though particular dogs are apt to play too long and exhaust themselves galivanting about and not minding the business . . . though all things considered there is nothing like paying homage to and teasing a young bitch for whetting her appetite. Of course the dear girl may have someone else in mind and just will not let the selected dog serve her, and may if she is an expert at dropping her rear suddenly at the critical moment tire the dog out or cause him to ejaculate outside the vagina, in either of which cases the mating will have to be postponed until the next day.

Now and then it happens that a bitch will not be served willingly and has to be held for the dog, and on top of that may have to be taped or muzzled while being served. Certainly she should be taped if really bad tempered. One good method is to bind a two-inch bandage several times round the jaws with the ends crossing underneath and then passing to and around the neck where they can be securely tied. A string tied tightly round the muzzle is not really good ; and in any case what with saliva dribbles and froth blowings you would have an awful job undoing the thing anyway. Another rather kind binder is a length of soft sheepskin (say two or three inches wide of the kind used for making shopping bags and bellows) with strong tapes attached to holes at the ends, which can be wound round and round the jaws and fastened with the tapes as in the bandage method.

The normal mating will look after itself well enough, but now and then control of a fractious bitch is called for, for without actually being snappy an unwilling bitch can delay the service no end. Those who drop their rears can have them supported by the hand through pressure with the palm upward from below the loins. The bitches who flip their tails down for coverage should have these held to one side well out of the way. All these little things may never crop up, but if they do then it is necessary to help the stud. The stud himself may need help if he is young or disinterested, or though keen to try just unable to effect entry with that particular bitch. Stimulation by voice and a firm scratch or two down the lower spine may help enough, but now and again it may be necessary for direct positive help in effecting an entry and seeing that everything functions once started. If the bitch is small and a maiden a smear of 'Vaseline' will help a lot. If the stud is small in build generally and the bitch high on her hindquarters the dog can be built up by raising the level of the floor below his hindquarters—a rough copra mat gives his feet as good a grip as anything.

Service is almost always sealed with a close physical juxtaposition commonly called the tie. In a small handbook like this we need not go into the mechanics of this device of Nature nor need we deal with its complications for all these things are described in detail in my general work *The Dog Breeder's Manual* (Sampson Low & Co.). Not all breeds tie, and not all individual dogs in the tying breeds tie, so no serious alarm should arise at not finding a stud tying. For my own part I prefer to see a good tie, not the prolonged affairs of an hour or so, but at least a definite tie of a dozen minutes or so. In any case on the establishment of a tie the breeder has visible evidence that a service is being fully given, and he can testify to that effect.

What to do during the tie occasionally worries some breeders of little experience, and I would advise them not to meddle at all except in such unusual cases where help is obviously required. Once the tie is effected in full the dog's forequarters (and his weight) should be shed from the bitch and the dogs turned back to back in the usual way.

It is not essential but I think it a good plan with any long-coated breed of dog to have the stud lightly sponged around the genitals to remove any trace of his having just been mated before putting him back in the kennels. Other males may well be jealous of his activity or at least excited by the smell he would carry back with him if not wiped down with a mild disinfectant. A sponge dipped in diluted 'Dettol' is excellent for the purpose; in any case such a practice serves to disinfect a valuable stud after service with a strange bitch. Finally, for the sake of peace and quiet in the kennels it is wiser, if the stud concerned lives with others in a large kennel range, to put him for a while into a separate kennel until he is settled and no longer feeling a cut above the others.

## WHELPING

The bitch in whelp should be kept in tip-top condition throughout her pregnancy, as sound puppies cannot be produced out of an unsound dam. Gestation is a most important time and never in the entire nine weeks of it should the in-whelp bitch be allowed to fall off in condition. The second half is more important and it is then when extra nourishment is certainly necessary. Fussing over an in-whelp bitch during the first month of pregnancy is entirely unnecessary, and indeed it is likely to upset the bitch if she is a maiden or nervous. To see she does not fight, stuff or starve herself, or become infested with worms is about all you need worry about at that time.

Gestation is usually from sixty to sixty-five days ; and which day whelping will take place can rarely be determined with accuracy. The chart on page 62 is a guide worked out on the sixty-three day basis which may help in marking your whelping calendar. Environment begins in the womb, so instead of waiting for the puppies to arrive, take cod liver oil and other aids to bone and tissue formation and give them to them while being formed in the womb through the mother. Give the bitch additional sources of nourishment during this time, at latest towards the second month of the gestation: calcium phosphate or calcium lactate, halibut or cod liver oil, dried brewer's yeast, tomato juices, and other rich sources are invaluable. As the meals become a shade larger it is better, of course, to stagger them and feed little and often so not to expand the stomach too much—once she begins to barrel out there will be little room for expansion of her stomach anyway.

Some bitches button themselves up even to the last but generally they show a barrelling of the body about the sixth week or so, and the teats will follow with enlargement, and later still the characteristic rolling gait will show all is well on the way. By the time she has been pregnant for close on two months the puppies can with luck be felt and some idea of their number worked out, that is, if the bitch is not abnormally fat or the litter a large one of puny mites. About then is the

### TABLE SHOWING WHEN A BITCH IS DUE TO WHELP

| Served Jan. | Whelps March | Served Feb. | Whelps April | Served March | Whelps May | Served April | Whelps June | Served May | Whelps July | Served June | Whelps Aug | Served July | Whelps Sept. | Served Aug | Whelps Oct. | Served Sept. | Whelps Nov. | Served Oct. | Whelps Dec. | Served Nov. | Whelps Jan. | Served Dec. | Whelps Feb. |
|---|---|---|---|---|---|---|---|---|---|---|---|---|---|---|---|---|---|---|---|---|---|---|---|
| 1 | 5 | 1 | 5 | 1 | 3 | 1 | 3 | 1 | 3 | 1 | 3 | 1 | 2 | 1 | 3 | 1 | 3 | 1 | 3 | 1 | 3 | 1 | 2 |
| 2 | 6 | 2 | 6 | 2 | 4 | 2 | 4 | 2 | 4 | 2 | 4 | 2 | 3 | 2 | 4 | 2 | 4 | 2 | 4 | 2 | 4 | 2 | 3 |
| 3 | 7 | 3 | 7 | 3 | 5 | 3 | 5 | 3 | 5 | 3 | 5 | 3 | 4 | 3 | 5 | 3 | 5 | 3 | 5 | 3 | 5 | 3 | 4 |
| 4 | 8 | 4 | 8 | 4 | 6 | 4 | 6 | 4 | 6 | 4 | 6 | 4 | 5 | 4 | 6 | 4 | 6 | 4 | 6 | 4 | 6 | 4 | 5 |
| 5 | 9 | 5 | 9 | 5 | 7 | 5 | 7 | 5 | 7 | 5 | 7 | 5 | 6 | 5 | 7 | 5 | 7 | 5 | 7 | 5 | 7 | 5 | 6 |
| 6 | 10 | 6 | 10 | 6 | 8 | 6 | 8 | 6 | 8 | 6 | 8 | 6 | 7 | 6 | 8 | 6 | 8 | 6 | 8 | 6 | 8 | 6 | 7 |
| 7 | 11 | 7 | 11 | 7 | 9 | 7 | 9 | 7 | 9 | 7 | 9 | 7 | 8 | 7 | 9 | 7 | 9 | 7 | 9 | 7 | 9 | 7 | 8 |
| 8 | 12 | 8 | 12 | 8 | 10 | 8 | 10 | 8 | 10 | 8 | 10 | 8 | 9 | 8 | 10 | 8 | 10 | 8 | 10 | 8 | 10 | 8 | 9 |
| 9 | 13 | 9 | 13 | 9 | 11 | 9 | 11 | 9 | 11 | 9 | 11 | 9 | 10 | 9 | 11 | 9 | 11 | 9 | 11 | 9 | 11 | 9 | 10 |
| 10 | 14 | 10 | 14 | 10 | 12 | 10 | 12 | 10 | 12 | 10 | 12 | 10 | 11 | 10 | 12 | 10 | 12 | 10 | 12 | 10 | 12 | 10 | 11 |
| 11 | 15 | 11 | 15 | 11 | 13 | 11 | 13 | 11 | 13 | 11 | 13 | 11 | 12 | 11 | 13 | 11 | 13 | 11 | 13 | 11 | 13 | 11 | 12 |
| 12 | 16 | 12 | 16 | 12 | 14 | 12 | 14 | 12 | 14 | 12 | 14 | 12 | 13 | 12 | 14 | 12 | 14 | 12 | 14 | 12 | 14 | 12 | 13 |
| 13 | 17 | 13 | 17 | 13 | 15 | 13 | 15 | 13 | 15 | 13 | 15 | 13 | 14 | 13 | 15 | 13 | 15 | 13 | 15 | 13 | 15 | 13 | 14 |
| 14 | 18 | 14 | 18 | 14 | 16 | 14 | 16 | 14 | 16 | 14 | 16 | 14 | 15 | 14 | 16 | 14 | 16 | 14 | 16 | 14 | 16 | 14 | 15 |
| 15 | 19 | 15 | 19 | 15 | 17 | 15 | 17 | 15 | 17 | 15 | 17 | 15 | 16 | 15 | 17 | 15 | 17 | 15 | 17 | 15 | 17 | 15 | 16 |
| 16 | 20 | 16 | 20 | 16 | 18 | 16 | 18 | 16 | 18 | 16 | 18 | 16 | 17 | 16 | 18 | 16 | 18 | 16 | 18 | 16 | 18 | 16 | 17 |
| 17 | 21 | 17 | 21 | 17 | 19 | 17 | 19 | 17 | 19 | 17 | 19 | 17 | 18 | 17 | 19 | 17 | 19 | 17 | 19 | 17 | 19 | 17 | 18 |
| 18 | 22 | 18 | 22 | 18 | 20 | 18 | 20 | 18 | 20 | 18 | 20 | 18 | 19 | 18 | 20 | 18 | 20 | 18 | 20 | 18 | 20 | 18 | 19 |
| 19 | 23 | 19 | 23 | 19 | 21 | 19 | 21 | 19 | 21 | 19 | 21 | 19 | 20 | 19 | 21 | 19 | 21 | 19 | 21 | 19 | 21 | 19 | 20 |
| 20 | 24 | 20 | 24 | 20 | 22 | 20 | 22 | 20 | 22 | 20 | 22 | 20 | 21 | 20 | 22 | 20 | 22 | 20 | 22 | 20 | 22 | 20 | 21 |
| 21 | 25 | 21 | 25 | 21 | 23 | 21 | 23 | 21 | 23 | 21 | 23 | 21 | 22 | 21 | 23 | 21 | 23 | 21 | 23 | 21 | 23 | 21 | 22 |
| 22 | 26 | 22 | 26 | 22 | 24 | 22 | 24 | 22 | 24 | 22 | 24 | 22 | 23 | 22 | 24 | 22 | 24 | 22 | 24 | 22 | 24 | 22 | 23 |
| 23 | 27 | 23 | 27 | 23 | 25 | 23 | 25 | 23 | 25 | 23 | 25 | 23 | 24 | 23 | 25 | 23 | 25 | 23 | 25 | 23 | 25 | 23 | 24 |
| 24 | 28 | 24 | 28 | 24 | 26 | 24 | 26 | 24 | 26 | 24 | 26 | 24 | 25 | 24 | 26 | 24 | 26 | 24 | 26 | 24 | 26 | 24 | 25 |
| 25 | 29 | 25 | 29 | 25 | 27 | 25 | 27 | 25 | 27 | 25 | 27 | 25 | 26 | 25 | 27 | 25 | 27 | 25 | 27 | 25 | 27 | 25 | 26 |
| 26 | 30 | 26 | 30 | 26 | 28 | 26 | 28 | 26 | 28 | 26 | 28 | 26 | 27 | 26 | 28 | 26 | 28 | 26 | 28 | 26 | 28 | 26 | 27 |
| 27 | 31 | 27 | 1 | 27 | 29 | 27 | 29 | 27 | 29 | 27 | 29 | 27 | 28 | 27 | 29 | 27 | 29 | 27 | 29 | 27 | 29 | 27 | 28 |
| 28 | 1 | 28 | 2 | 28 | 30 | 28 | 30 | 28 | 30 | 28 | 30 | 28 | 29 | 28 | 30 | 28 | 30 | 28 | 30 | 28 | 30 | 28 | 1 |
| 29 | 2 | 29 | 3 | 29 | 31 | 29 | 1 | 29 | 31 | 29 | 31 | 29 | 30 | 29 | 31 | 29 | 1 | 29 | 31 | 29 | 31 | 29 | 2 |
| 30 | 3 | | | 30 | 1 | 30 | 2 | 30 | 1 | 30 | 1 | 30 | 1 | 30 | 1 | 30 | 2 | 30 | 1 | 30 | 1 | 30 | 3 |
| 31 | 4 | | | 31 | 2 | | | 31 | 2 | | | 31 | 2 | 31 | 2 | | | 31 | 2 | | | 31 | 4 |

time to get her whelping box ready, or at least some quiet spot in the kennels away from other bitches if not away from all the other dogs. Be sure her whelping box is large enough to be comfortable in moving about (for she will fidget a good deal) but small enough to be cosy. The floor can be covered with a piece of hessian or clean sacking which should be tacked firmly all round its edges after being stretched tight. Around the inner walls strong metal bars or lengths of deal say about 2 inches by 2 inches can be fastened to take the inexperienced dam's weight off the puppies so that in turning around she cannot lie on them and smother them. And it is time too to see the first-aid kit is handy. What your kit is depends on what you believe necessary, of course, but the out-and-out novice would be wise to have say the following:

> a dozen soft paper napkins or 9 in. squares of lint
> a pair of sharp and clean probe-pointed surgical scissors
> some surgical thread or strong cotton
> ' Vaseline '
> ' Dettol '
> ' T.C.P.', or similar disinfectant
> some dry pieces of rough towelling
> a covered hot water bottle
> an emergency feeding bottle
> a few drops of brandy or other spirits

The last-minute signs are generally well known but to go over them briefly does no harm: the bitch usually becomes fretful and anxious, and may lose her appetite just towards the end of term; her external genitals will swell, and there will be a discharge of mucus; she will check her whelping bed over herself and arrange its bedding to suit herself and not her owner; she will strain her head round looking anxiously at her rear now and then and may whimper. In practically every case the actual labour is about due when these signs are evident, and she should be watched carefully. Usually the whelping begins with rather gentle muscular contractions which seem to ripple down the whole body, and then occur in increasing strength and frequency until the contractions are really powerful. If she pants a lot in between the bearing-down strains you can let her have a small drink of warm milk, or her favourite warm drink, but do not interfere otherwise. If the straining goes on for quite a time, in the regular rhythm which usually heralds the birth of the first puppy, without results you had better get veterinary help quickly; as would be the case too if she is unusually late in term, say the sixty-fifth day.

Puppies are born one at a time each in its own membranous sac. This is common knowledge among experienced breeders, of course, but I *have* known a novice begin breeding expecting the bitch's litter to arrive all at once in one container (and such an idea is to my mind quite forgivable). The usual presentation is with the head and forefeet first, and this is so common that it is not necessary here to discuss the other presentations. Meddling during whelping is most undesirable: with Bulldogs, Pekingese, and certain other breeds help is necessary quite often due to the abnormality of the large head and small pubic aperture, but with Afghans there is no excuse for fiddling about and interfering with Nature's own course. If the bitch is a maiden, if she is really small and appears to have a large and exhausting litter, if the first puppy is stranded half way down the passage, or any similar trouble is indicated, *then* human assistance is warranted. The average Afghan bitch is a good mother and works energetically delivering, severing the cords and opening the sacs readily, and cleaning up all round nicely ; lazy or vicious bitches want watching and help must then be given in the interests of the puppies, but apart from these unusual cases it is far better not to fuss around her at that time.

A maiden bitch is usually the one who demands attention for she tends to panic at times, especially when the litter is numerous and the deliveries appear to be going on for ever. She gets quite nervy and needs comforting, and in such a case it is better and kinder to do some of her work for her. The first puppy may hurt tremendously and the bitch may tire before its delivery ; if it protrudes while the strainings are continuing even if weak it can be gripped with one of the pieces of rough towelling and gently drawn out *during the strains*. The bitch usually releases the puppy from the bag, severs the cord and cleans up, but again if it appears necessary the breeder can do this with the scissors and lint squares in the kit. The cords need not be severed too hurriedly, and in fact do no harm if left a few minutes as long as they do not tighten and pull from the puppy thus inducing umbilical hernia. Afterbirths are expelled separately, one after each puppy. The flow of blood from the placenta (or afterbirth) to the puppy deteriorates quickly and so if the cord is allowed to stay a while, say as long as it takes to clean the puppy with the towelling and stimulate it into crying by a little friction, the chances of heavy bleeding are much reduced. To unpack each pup from its container is far more important than hanging around with scissors at the ready for cord snipping. As already said, the bitch generally does everything herself using Nature's instruments of teeth and tongue. When it is really necessary to snip the cord cut some half-inch or so from the puppy's navel and tie tightly with the surgical thread or cotton in the kit as a ligature. Some bitches eat the afterbirths (it is perfectly natural for them, being a habit formed in the wild state when a warm meal had to be taken in times when it was dangerous for the mother to go hunting and leave the puppies unprotected), but some breeders stop them doing so as they may have upset tummies as a result in these no longer wild days—then that is a question on which there are many opinions.

Generally puppies are born in fairly quick succession, the second following the afterbirth of the first and so on ; the intervals between each puppy may be from two or three minutes to an hour or more but half an hour is reasonable. Long time lags accompanied by straining mean the veterinary surgeon may be needed, as would an abnormally large number of puppies. When the litter is a large one and you see that all the pups cannot be accommodated in the whelping box put the extras into another bed with the covered hot water bottle. Do not overlook the final afterbirth, for if this is not forthcoming in reasonable time better call veterinary help and douch the bitch with warm water to which a suspicion of ' Dettol ' has been added.

After everything is finished give the bitch a drink of warm milk (a beaten egg or a little glucose added helps a lot) and let or lead her out to relieve herself. While she is away from the puppies these can be gone over for deformities (including cleft palate among the obvious ones), and checked for sexes, and the bed renewed ready for the dam's return.

Normally the dam will begin to suckle the puppies easily enough, and there should be enough milk for the ordinary litter. The usual number of teats is eight; sometimes there are more or less than eight, and uncommonly there is an odd number of teats. Many teats do not mean more milk or even more taps for the puppies to turn on, for the pectoral or brisket teats rarely yield much though the inguinal or groin teats are invariably generous. Keep the timid babies at the inguinal teats and the gluttons at others *if* you can . . . the strong ones usually fight their way to the best spots at the expense of the weaker or quieter ones. Do not forget the nursing bitch needs extra nourishment herself and lots of liquids. Watch her well at this time, and if she seems annoyed with the pups shortly check them over for sharp nails, and see her teats are not dry and sore.

If you think the litter too large for the bitch to feed herself then a foster mother should be had to help out with the mothering. Where a bitch is habitually a poor mother you will, of course, have advance notice enough to arrange that a foster reaches your kennels in time for the whelping and to take over most of the feeding. Fosters should be had from clean kennels advertising in the dog journals (*Dog World* and *Our Dogs*), and in booking a foster particulars of whelping dates and so on should be given. Remember too that even if the foster is seen on arrival to be of third-class breeding she will still yield a first-class milk, and, if you time your litters right, she can help out with the surplus pups of two of your bitches.

As Afghan bitches generally have rather large litters

in any case, and on top of that are liable to ruin their coats if trying to feed all their pups, it is a good plan to have a permanent foster in the kennels of some large breed or other. This foster can then take on say a half of the puppies and so save at least some of the mess which the Afghan bitch would otherwise get herself into.

In almost all breeds it is possible for a bitch to have a false pregnancy but somehow I suspect the Afghan has a weakness for this sort of tomfoolery, often carrying the effect to the extreme. False pregnancies are nothing new at all. M. de Mailly, of the Academy of Dijon, told Buffon (in a letter dated 6th October 1772) about a bitch belonging to the curate of Norges (near Dijon) who ' without either having ever been pregnant, or delivered of puppies, had all the symptoms which characterize these two states. She came into season at the usual period ; but never had any connections with a male. When the common term of gestation was finished, her paps were distended with milk . . . suckled some young puppies with which she was furnished, and for whom she discovered as much tenderness and attention as if she had been their real mother '. This same bitch similarly suckled two kittens in 1769. So, as I say, this result of a bitch's wishful thinking is not at all new. Miss M. C. Mathews' " Feathers " was a case in point: she would almost at the sight of puppies rally her milk supplies and offer herself as a foster at every opportunity! Mrs. Trudi Guberlet of Washington (who is about to publish a book of Afghan caricatures, with comments, of her Afghan bitch " Khazeeda Hafsa el Myia ") tells me in a most amusing letter that: ' " Khazeeda ", with typical feminine

Plate XIII

Miss Eileen Snelling with her
" Sirdar of Khorrassan ",
then a puppy of five months.

Mrs. Sydney Rhodes'
head kennel-maid
with Ch. " Ajawaan
Chita Mia ".

*Photo by Sheffield Telegraph*

Two post-war
Champion bitches,
" Ajawaan Chita
Mia " and " Ajawaan
Rani Tamba ".

*Photo by Sheffield Telegraph.*

Plate XIV

*(right)*
  Mrs. Trudi Guberlet's
 "Khazeeda Hafsa El Myia".

    *Photo by Hopper.*

*(below)*
  Mrs. Molly Sharpe's
 "Garrymhor Faiz-Bu-Hassid"
   racing.

*Photo by Scottish Pictorial Press.*

"Turkuman
 Nissim's Laurel"
photographed before
export to the U.S.A.

   *Photo by Fall.*

jealousy, decided a few months ago that her daughters received entirely too much limelight and so she chose to pull a false pregnancy on me. She accomplished the desired effect in that I believed her. My belief entailed copious amounts of eggs, thick cream, new sleeping quarters, a flurry of knitting. Right up to the supposedly crucial hour—then I knew '.

If you decide to remove the dew-claws do so within a day or two of birth. Some breeders wait four or five days but I think it is kinder to remove them on the second day. Ordinary scissors will do if nice and sharp, but docking scissors are better, if you hold them half open, and insert the entire digit in the circular aperture and press the blades close into the side of the leg. Dab afterwards with Friar's Balsam or a few crushed crystals of permanganate of potassium.

# CHAPTER VI

## FEEDING

WEANING can begin when the puppies are about a month old, where the litter is of average size and the dam in good condition. If the dam is doing very well and the family thriving then it can start a little later . . . while the supply is there it may as well be allowed to the pups, for there is no milk quite so good.

A prepared liquid puppy food of any well-known brand or a raw egg beaten in milk can be the first food a puppy can be taught to lap, and it should be given as a change or relief meal rather than as a staple diet during the fourth week. For the first few days a few teaspoonfuls would be enough to begin with, and then the amount can be increased gradually. Tomato juice and halibut liver oil can be added once or twice a week and make welcome changes in flavour. After a few days a little scraped raw meat can be fed, moistened with cod liver oil. By the fifth week the puppies can be having half their feed from their dam and half from the dish, the amount of solids being gradually increased all the time, until by the sixth week the number of dish feeds can be raised to about six meals daily, each of a very small quantity of course, and the bitch's milk given only during the night if it is needed. The solids can include steamed fish with crumbled stale wheatmeal or brown bread (avoid white bread unless baked again), or such crumbs with a good non-salty meat extract. The puppies should still be kept with their dam at night at least until she is dried out, and they are big enough to do without her warmth.

Goat's milk is an excellent help if the bitch runs dry very early, and in any case helps tremendously in rearing strong puppies. In fact the value of fresh goat's milk can hardly be overstressed in view of its high fat and mineral salts contents, and, of course, its general freedom from tubercular contamination. It has taken a long time for general appreciation of its value but more and more of the successful breeders are keeping a goat or two specially for puppy and invalid feeding: when I was with the 'Ivanhoe' boarding kennels and the 'Lanarth' Wires years before the Second World War I always used goat's milk, and never was a weakling raised in either kennels. Incidentally, as very few of the branded puppy foods so popular years ago have as yet returned on the market it is all the more necessary to use the richest natural sources obtainable. Milk puddings made with cow's milk, and starchy foods like biscuit meals and so on, can be given when the puppies have got well under way—there is no point in rushing these during the first few weeks of weaning. And cow's milk should in any case be strengthened with say a plasmon or casein preparation or a full-cream milk powder: it should *never* be diluted.

An appreciation of the great differences between

bitch's milk and that of goats and cows is made easier by the analyses published in *The Dog Breeder's Manual* (Sampson Low & Co.). Here is the table:

ANALYSIS OF MILK

| Animal | Sugar | Casein, etc. | Fat | Salts | Water |
|--------|-------|--------------|-----|-------|-------|
| Dog | 3.1 | 8.0 | 12.0 | 1.2 | 75.5 |
| Goat | 4.75 | 4.0 | 6.25 | 1.0 | 84.0 |
| Cat | 5.2 | 7.9 | 3.65 | 0.9 | 82.35 |
| Cow | 4.85 | 3.75 | 3.7 | 0.6 | 87.1 |
| Sheep | 4.95 | 4.7 | 5.2 | 0.7 | 84.45 |

When the puppies are about two months old the mincer can be used for the meat, instead of hand scraping the lean away from the sinews, but until about the seventh week scraping is much better. From the ninth or tenth week even the mincing machine can be dispensed with, and meat cut into small lumps. Grated raw carrots and sieved tomatoes are useful flavourers in the puppy meals, and as regulators a little stewed fruit or liver (raw against constipation: cooked against looseness) can be added when necessary. A miss in meals now and then with a cleansing by minced raw garlic or garlic oil will do more good than generally imagined ; and do not overlook the value of specific herbal feeding. Greens can be added for body when the puppies are two to three months old and should not be hurried upon them as long as there are meat, eggs, fish, milk and special puppy meal available.

While weaning off give all feeds warm, even of liquids. The first feeds can be say twice a day while the puppy is with the bitch and sucking, then increased to four or five while the bitch gives less milk, then when completely weaned they can be raised to eight daily. On reaching the sixth week they can be reduced to seven slightly larger meals, and at the eighth week to six meals, the first being given nice and early and the last really late, with a generous gap in the afternoon so the puppy can have as much rest as he needs then. At this age milk puddings and cereal dishes can be given to help out the meat and fish meals.

## PUPPY FEEDING

By the time a puppy is two months old he should have forgotten all about his mother's breasts and so should his breeder. In fact he should be quite weaned off by the sixth week, though sometimes it is earlier still and sometimes later. At two months he should be gradually getting on to solid stuff and having his meals at say 7 a.m., 10 a.m., 1 p.m., 4 p.m., 7 p.m. and 10 p.m. Two weeks later the last meal can be dropped, and the remaining five meals fed at say 8 a.m., 11 a.m., 2 p.m., 6 p.m., and 9 p.m. Another fortnight makes the puppy three months old and then he can do with about four rather more substantial meals given say at 8 a.m., 12 noon, 4 p.m., and some time in the evening. Such a programme of feeding can in most cases continue (with the quantities being increased of course) until the puppy is five or six months old, when another meal can be dropped and the three left him fed morning, noon and evening, say about 8 a.m., 12 noon, and about 6 p.m. When he is about ten months old two good feeds daily should suffice, if they have as much nourishment as body of course, and due regard is given to the fact that the dog is still not quite mature and needs help. Therefore there must be a big difference between the two meals given a ten-months youngster and those fed a mature adult.

By now you should be selling off your surplus stock, for they should be shaping out at say from two-and-a-half to three months, and although you do not want to have them hanging on until half-grown, eating more and more food every day, you cannot possibly let them go until well weaned off and having a decent start for their future lives. If you keep them too long they will not sell so readily, and your costs may outweigh most of their price when you do dispose of them, yet if you sell them too early they may not thrive, and would in the long run do your kennel and reputation harm.

The puppy of two or three months can be helped so much by good feeding that it is worth while paying special attention to the diet at that age. Remember raw eggs are extremely valuable and even the small breeder should not overlook the great help they give in building up a young puppy; he can so easily buy a quantity during the glut period and pickle them for emergency or winter use in a large earthenware vessel. Dried yeast is also a very great help in puppyhood. The bakers' yeast is nothing like so good as dried brewers' yeast, which when fresh is about the richest natural source of vitamin B that it is possible to get at all. 'Vetzyme' is really dried brewers' yeast, but concentrated with supplementary minerals specially for dogs. Other helps are Parrish's chemical food and Easton's syrup, which are good all-round iron tonics, the

first often liked by dogs, but the second not at all liked
owing to its strychnine bitterness (you can give it in
capsule form now). Calcium in tabloid form helps for
bone building, but it is by no means an indispensable
adjunct in the kennel kitchen. Honey can be made use
of during extreme puppyhood or in illness, when with
warm milk it is most beneficial.

Meat and fish are invaluable. If the meat is scraped
for the really small puppies the waste sinews and so on
can be put into the stewpot for thickening the broth
for the grown dogs, as can the bones, cartilage and fat
pieces. By the way, meat is better fed large enough to
give the dog some work for his jaws, so once the dog is
out of early puppyhood dispense with the mincing
machine and cut the meat into chunks not smaller than
say an ' Oval ' or ' Shape ' biscuit. Fish must be carefully cleaned of sharp penetrating bones, and dried
salted fish should not be used for puppy feeding—for
that matter salted fish is not really good for adult dogs
either, especially if given to dogs liable to skin
troubles.

Greens are really good once the puppy is past the
critical age, say two to three months, when the starchy
foods and root vegetables can be fed without any worry.
Fresh greens are rich in mineral salts and some of them
can be fed chopped up raw, such as spinach and lettuce.
Others need cooking, especially kale and turnip-tops
(these latter are rich in iodine and though not often
appreciated they deserve more use). Young nettle
leaves are another valuable source of nutriment, when
cooked gently. Roots like carrots, parsnips and turnips
are good sources of vitamin C, and can be given minced
raw or cooked. Peas and beans have good protein value

and are enjoyed now and then as mixers in the food.
The onion family are, of course, excellent generally,
and its members can be grated raw into the food now
and then, as can celery also.   Meat, fish, fruit, root
vegetables and greenstuffs will together supply plenty
of protein and fat to the growing puppy.   His starch
requirements will easily be satisfied with his biscuit
meal, crumbled wholemeal bread or rusks, sago or
tapioca puddings, barley and maize meal ;  these fillers
usually come along so readily that you need really only
worry about getting the right amount of protein and fat
into the body.

## ADULT FEEDING

Some dogs mature quicker than others, of course, but
once the growing dog has got to the stage where he has
two meals a day he can stay at that number of feeds,
though the morning meal can be reduced to a mere
snack when the dog has finished growing.   Stud dogs
and brood bitches naturally need extra nourishment
but the ordinary adult does not really need more than
a really good nourishing evening meal with a snack
during the morning.

Again with the adult dogs the three constituents of
their food must be protein, fat and starch, in order to
build up and replace worn out tissue, to maintain a
healthy temperature, and to give energy, respectively.
These builders, warmers and energisers are found in all
the foods I have already mentioned in dealing with
puppy feeding, and when mineral salts and water are
added all in their right proportions adult dogs should in

all ordinary circumstances certainly be healthy and well conditioned. In a little book like this it is not necessary to talk about the vitamins each in turn, and how they can be given the dogs, for much of this is common knowledge and if it is not then I refer you to my *Dog Breeder's Manual*.

What I have already said of meat and fish in puppy feeding applies equally in adult feeding, and meat here means not only muscular tissue but kidneys, liver, paunches, chitterlings, and in fact all the viscera. It will be a long time before we can buy sheep's paunches for 2d. again (certainly not during the time of the Welfare State), but whatever the cost may be when you can get them they make excellent food: messy to clean perhaps, but every bit meat without waste. Butcher's scraps too are well worth acquiring, as are fishmonger's scraps. Cods' heads when boiled make a tasty meal with Terrier or Hound meal added to the broth, though there is much work in taking out the innumerable bones. More nourishing fish though a little dearer are fresh herrings and mackerel. These are both really excellent foods, especially the mackerel. Herrings are cheap enough during glut periods and should certainly be fed then if not during the entire season. Cods' roes are nourishing as are those of any fish. Sardines in oil or tomato juice give flavour, break the monotony of ordinary feeding, and tone up the system as well; invalids and breeding dogs need them from time to time.

Greens, root vegetables and some cereals have already been mentioned, but remember if a dog particularly likes fruit then let him have it when available. Many dogs will prowl the garden specially in search of berries and fallen apples, and these are all quite good for them. Of course other dogs will go on the prowl for not so pleasant things like eggshells or dung, and then you realize that the food being fed them is deficient in mineral salts.

Biscuits are generally fed dry during the morning or midday snack meal, and these can range according to individual taste from 'Ovals', 'Shapes', 'Marvels' and the like to the really big square cakes which give the teeth something hard to work on. These biscuits can also be used as rewards during training, hunting or at play. The biscuit for the evening meal is usually fed soaked, and this is done an hour or so before feeding time by pouring sufficient really hot broth or stock over the measured biscuit meal to allow it to plim up and absorb the broth. If the biscuit meal is measured out into a large bowl, the broth poured over, and left to stand until cool enough for feeding, it will be fairly soft; this helps in so much that if the biscuit must plim at all it is far better it does this outside the dogs than inside, and so it is the usual practice for all biscuit meals from fine to coarse to be swollen by absorption of a good nourishing gravy. Considering that the evening biscuit meal is softened it is therefore wiser to give a pretty coarse-grained meal, keeping the finer grades for puppies and invalids.

Bones and water are on the face of things easy enough to get and to give yet so many people overlook the necessity for giving them while fresh. Evil-smelling bones and stale water do not contribute to soundness in dogs any more than in humans, although it is true some dogs like their meal and bones a trifle high. Puppies especially need their water changing very often; and the in-whelp bitch seems never to find a bottom to her drinking bowl. Incidentally, neither the dogs nor I will thank people who put sticks of rock sulphur in the water bowl.

The feeding of raw food has rightly attracted some attention lately, and I have always advocated the feeding of raw meat wherever possible, and, too, the giving of raw grated root vegetables, some fruits, and greens like minced celery, garlic, spinach, and lettuce. Robust country-bred dogs are often fed whole rabbits (or at least a share of a whole rabbit) and appear to enjoy eating the entire animal, fur, feet, viscera and everything complete. The meat is fresh, the valuable blood is obtained, and the worrying and breaking up of the animal gives the teeth work and the dog considerable pleasure. Against these advantages do not forget the fact that in spring and summer very many rabbits have their furs literally alive with fleas, and almost all the year round some rabbits are infested with tapeworms—fleas and tapeworms go well together of course, but neither should be welcome on or in the dogs. Herrings fed raw are excellent too, but let them be proportionate in size to the dogs eating them: a tough dog can manage a full-sized herring perhaps, but let the sprat of a dog tackle a sprat of a herring—a few of those are quite enough. Mackerel is excellent raw, but not in its entirety, as the bones are so powerful, so it is much better to fillet them first and pop the waste into a pot for broth over the evening meal of biscuit.

# CHAPTER VII

## MANAGEMENT

THE successful management of dogs depends, of course, upon a number of factors of which the most important are how the dogs are housed and fed. Feeding is so often regarded as much more a complicated subject than it really need be that I have dealt with it on its own in the preceding chapter, but there still remain a few other important points to run over which are contributing factors to good management.

Housing means, of course, giving the dogs proper shelter, which may mean that they are kept indoors or out in specially constructed kennels or outhouses—that is a subject we shall consider presently. And then on top of feeding and housing comes conditioning, which though largely dependent upon food and shelter relies too upon the attentions given to grooming and exercise, and immediate treatment for internal and external troubles.

In order to have immediate treatment when needed you should make friends with your veterinary surgeon ; have him give the kennels a periodical run over, and consult him when in doubt about any problem worrying you.

## KENNELLING

The situation, size and number of kennels you have depends upon the average total of dogs in your care. If you have only one or two, as have very many novice breeders, you may keep them in the house, properly house-trained and generally given the run of the home but sleeping in proper dog pens of the double or single type made by well-known kennel makers. In fact quite a few very experienced breeders keep an old stud or brood matron in the house, or perhaps a retired show dog ; and really, apart from a very slight tendency towards fatness of the dogs concerned through getting extra titbits now and then, those dogs kept in the house do very well indeed.

But where the dogs are many in number, or where it is inconvenient to keep the two or three you may have in the house, outside kennels are the only solution to the housing problem, whether these are converted stables or outhouses, or home-made affairs of some kind, or properly constructed kennel ranges. Where the dogs are kept in outside kennels it does, however, pay to see that these are the best you can afford and in keeping with the quality of your stock. Far better a few good dogs in good kennels than masses of mediocres in ramshackle affairs.

Few breeders are really able to choose beforehand the site for the kennels and work out to the last detail their building, but everyone should at least be able to determine a good spot from a bad one, and have an idea of what goes to make a serviceable kennel. There is, to begin with, more in it than the actual construction of the ranges or pens, for foundations, drainage, sunshine and shade, and other things all demand at least some attention. To run through these briefly, the foundations should be laid on a good soil, say a loam rather than a clay, covered with a healthy clover (stronger and more lasting than common grass), with perhaps a gentle slope towards the south or south-west. A gravel is quite good, of course, for it drains well, but as I said just now very few breeders can really pick their spot in advance, and have usually to do their best with what ground is available. Bad drainage means souring of the ground, which in turn may lead to ailments, and eventually to an overall loss in income. Facing the sun at its best or second best is for just as obvious reasons: a few kennels are built semicircular so that in facing outwards young stock can be moved from the east end to the west daily and so follow the sun, but for ordinary purposes where no great number of dogs are kept and room is valuable a straight range facing south is best. Some shade helps a lot, for in mid-summer puppies feel the heat rather severely, and welcome a shady patch in the exercise paddock. Therefore, a few trees (may as well be fruit trees as any other) or shrubs can be about the paddock ; and in playing puppies enjoy a dash through what vegetation there may be. People have mixed feelings about trees, I know, but as long as they are not whopping great elms or sycamores drip dripping all over the place after every shower I think a few do help to give some shade for the youngsters in the hottest periods.

The buildings themselves can be converted barns or stables, which by virtue of their usual roominess alone make cleaning a pleasant job, or the professionally constructed portable kennels sold by reputable firms. Now these wooden kennels are generally really sound affairs and as they can be bought to any of a wide number of specifications your particular requirements can be satisfied easily enough. The number needed depends, of course, on the number of dogs kept, but even in a small breeding establishment it is advisable to have one set aside as an isolation pen for sick cases, while in the larger places another can be used specially for whelping cases. Where you may have a roomy barn or outhouse and do not particularly wish to have it adapted although it may be spare then have one- two- or even three-room pens put into it for the dogs to sleep in, and use the floor of the building itself as an exercise yard in wet weather. Incidentally, if your exercising place is a yard of concrete, asphalt or brick then it is a good plan to put in a corner or two roomy wooden benches which are raised a little off the ground for the dogs to bask or rest on after running. A good strong clover stays sweet-smelling for a long time and wears well, and drains away nicely too, but just about as popular are the stone, brick or concrete yards which can be cleaned and disinfected so easily. These yards should have a gully and drain for quick drainage after hosing down, and puppies should never be let out in them until the surface is dry . . . a squeegee will dry up the concrete in very little time when used properly. On the whole a concrete surface is better than brick or asphalt, as it does not collect puddles of rain or urine, and dries off quicker in the sun too. Don't let puppies lie about on concrete in cold weather, but encourage them to use the wooden benches when they wish to rest.

Inside the kennels are the compartments for day and night use, or in practically all there are two sections which can be used this way in any case. The night or sleeping chamber should be made really comfortable, with a bedding suitable not only to the size of the dog but to the taste of the individual if you find one or two dogs have ideas of their own about bedding, as some do. In the day pen or indoor run a clean pine sawdust makes a good floor, as it absorbs urine and helps stools to be shovelled up easily—just a dusting over each, a little careful rolling in the sawdust and a smart shovelling, and the job is done. But in the sleeping part of the kennel a warm bedding is really needed. This can be of wood-wool, straw, or wood chips, but which you use depends a lot upon what knowledge you have gathered about the merits of each. I prefer wood-wool, those rather fine wood shavings sold in compressed bales of a cwt. or so, which when teazed out make a really soft and warm bed for any dog. Some people who have been in dogs longer than I prefer straw, and usually use the rye straw, as this does not encourage fleas so much as the others, but for a soft-skinned dog I still think the wood-wool kinder. But whatever bedding you use do not be too lavish with it, especially in summer, and if your beds are plain wooden boxes turned on their sides, or raised benches, then fix a sliding bedding board across the front to keep the bedding where it should be, or when the dog leaves his bed he will drag most of his bedding out.

The kennel equipment is something that tends to grow alarmingly and really does need a special store-

Plate XV

Mrs. Tønnessen's fine coated twelve-year-old bitch Nor.-Swed.Ch. "Kuranda".

Miss P. Burchett's "Kohistan Kassala of Palitana".

A Champion Afghan in the exercise run of the *Queen Elizabeth* liner.

*Cunard White Star.*

Plate XVI

*(right)*
Madge Titheradge, the actress,
with "Kym" in the play
"Theatre Royal" at the Lyric
Theatre, London, in 1935.

*Photo by George Dallison.*

*(below)*
A prize-winning picture by Max
Esper of Mrs. Ward Monroe
French with her Am.Chs.
"Windtryst's Afire" and
"Agha Kaimaakan of Arthea".

*Photo by Max Esper.*

cupboard if the kennels are self-contained ones, or possibly a whole room if the kennels run into a long
range. Cleaning gear like sweeping brushes, small
handbrushes, shovels, buckets, overalls, soaps and disinfectant should be kept away from the cooking and
grooming equipment. In the very small kennels the
cooking is done in the house but in the larger place a
cookhouse is needed and this should have pots and
pans, bins for storing biscuits and meal, meat and fish
safes, a large bowl for soaking meal in, plenty of feeding bowls of the type that does not tip easily, with
rather narrow ones for puppy feeding, large wooden
spoons and a knife or two, and many of the usual
kitchen utensils as well, including a mincing machine
with variable blades.

The general purpose equipment may include almost
anything, of course, depending on the size of the
kennels and your own ideas about what may be necessary. But one item I feel should be in every kennel,
and this is a fire extinguisher. Your dog breeding will
bring you a lot of sport, more hard work, and still more
headaches, before you reach the end ('for there is no
finality in dogs'—as Mr. Croxton Smith so rightly says)
. . . you should therefore take every sensible precaution
against fire. And remember, too, that if your kennels
consist of a big range using electric or gas light do see
you have a mains switch for them, and do see it is
used every night. If your place is without electricity or
gas, and you use hanging 'Aladdin' (or 'Tilley')
lamps then for goodness sake see the wicks are
properly trimmed, the oil is clean, that you have a
metal disc roof protection above each lamp, and after
turning them out at night wind the wicks up

again to make quite sure they have gone completely out.


## EXERCISE

The Afghan should never be allowed to go flabby through lack of exercise. Work and play contribute a great deal to the necessary toning up of the body (especially of the digestive system) and where dogs are not coursed in the country they should at least be encouraged to play vigorously, for leaping and climbing help so much more than ordinary walking, which is too often regarded as adequate exercise. The bitch heavy in whelp or heavy in milk is satisfied with a good walk and should be discouraged from violent activities, but for all other dogs there is no excuse for not giving adequate exercise.

The weather is not always kind, of course, so the times of exercise had better be arranged to suit the weather unless it looks as if the rain that started will be lasting the whole day, when rain or no rain the dogs must be taken outside if there is no barn or large covered run for them to play in. You can protect the dogs with dog macs if you wish, and for the fastidious there are rubber leggings, but for ordinary purposes as apart from cases of sickness where some exercise is vital I believe it much healthier to dispense with protective clothing altogether. Let the dogs get thoroughly wet and dry them just as thoroughly on return to the kennels . . . it will not hurt them in the least if in sound condition. Drying can be done in many ways: the slap up-to-date large kennels may have electric hair drying machines installed, such as are used in dog beauty parlours, and these are excellent ; next best is a rubbing down with a dry but rather coarse towel, but the snag here is that so often the handler passes from one dog to the next with the same old towel until the last dog in (probably the wettest) gets merely the surface wet off his coat. I have found one excellent way of drying a wet dog is to wet a chamois leather and wring it out very tightly and then wipe the dog down with it from head to feet following the lie of the hair, and if this does not completely dry or the dog begins shivering have a rather large and fairly deep box about a quarter filled with a coarse, clean sawdust (pine for preference) and standing the dog in it splash some sawdust over the body and rub it gently in the coat till what moisture remains has been absorbed. The sawdust can be brushed off very easily, and the whole job is much quicker than may at first appear. . . . I found that most dogs thoroughly enjoy this sort of dust bath, and some on returning from a wet walk would dash ahead and leap in the box and revel in it. So, whatever the weather be sure to exercise regularly.

## GROOMING AND BATHING

While exercise tones up the whole body a regular daily grooming acts as a tonic to the skin and its hair follicles, encouraging a healthy pelt and coat. Circulation can be toned up no end by proper grooming, and this helps not only to bring a bloom to the coat but to the superficial muscles as well.

Remember in grooming to spare the comb (especially

those merciless steel things) and spoil the brush. Combing at best leaves the hair woolly while if the coat is damp or has those moulting-period tangles it can do real damage: far better to work harder with a rather kind hairbrush, like a Maison Pearson, where the bristles are allowed some freedom. In damp weather grooming is essential in order to prevent felting of the trousers and long hair, but in dry weather it is a fair luxury to brush thoroughly say twice or thrice a week, not more. The heavily coated dogs need more brushing but except before shows this need not be excessive. Every breeder to his own fancy, of course ; for my own part I would far rather see owners keeping their dogs in show trim all the year round than undergrooming between shows and then trying desperately a day before the show to unmat, bath, brush and titivate what simply cannot be done in such short time.

If you like wearing or giving things made from dog wool then there is no problem of disposal of the combings. For many years now Afghan wool has been considered as fine as angora rabbit, and really soft knitwork can be made from it. Save your hair then, especially the long, soft and silky hair, and send it after sorting and washing carefully, to anyone you know who spins it into wool. The essential qualities are of course the good length of fibre, and the silky texture. When spun the wool can be natural or dyed turquoise, strawberry, blue, fawn and other shades, making lovely mittens, gloves, scarves and so on. Pomeranian, Pyrénean Mountain Dog (one breeder gets about 40 lb. a year from her giants), Chow Chow, Pekingese, Old English Sheepdog, Keeshond, and many other breeds all yield very good wool indeed ; the wool can be as fine as fine, yet of considerable body and durability. Miss M. C. Mathews ('Westover' kennels) is still taking in combings and making garments for people: her address is Westover, Church Stretton, Salop. Miss Mathews tells me that although Afghan is excellent wool to card and spin (she uses a two-ply to give strength) for gloves it is better if supported with a mixture of Keeshond or similar tough wool.* Another lady who for many years spun dog wool was Miss Lily Berry of Castle Hedingham. This lady is now Mrs. L. Marshall, and she still spins and knits dog-wool garments: her address is The Bridge House, Sible Hedingham, Essex.

But to return to grooming: sometimes breeders have asked for particulars of a good toilet powder. Baby and talcum powders are generally excellent, but before the Second World War I used on "Kym" a preparation which was if I recall it rightly made of oatmeal, borax and sulphur. I think the proportions were something like this:

8 oz. fine powdered oatmeal
2 oz. boracic powder
1 oz. flowers of sulphur.

This was properly mixed and kept in tins with tightly fitting but perforated lids, and a little shaken into the coat when brushing. Naturally such a preparation does the skin good as well as helping to separate the hair

---

* I have a pair of these gloves myself and find them beautifully warm and absolutely windproof. For a lone motorist or cyclist they are excellent: and if in jolly company they fluff your companion's navy blue suit you can truthfully blame the dog!

fibres and preventing felting, but might dull a glossy black dog if used liberally.

In grooming do not run quickly over the whole and do one part well, intending to do another part well to-morrow (plus a general lick and promise), rather as you might dust all the rooms in the house but turn out one properly—this system does not work so well with dogs. Better to take time and do the entire dog from head to tail, and then afterwards check again for teeth, eyes, ears, sores if any, vent and nails. It takes but a minute or two to run these extras over once you get used to it, and like the timely stitch you may this way save yourself no end of troubles later on. In the actual grooming remember to spare the steel comb (or any kind of comb for that matter) and spoil your brush, your Hound-glove or the palm of your hand. The more natural your grooming equipment the better will be the results . . . and of this the hand is possibly the best of all for imparting the last-minute gloss to a good healthy coat. You should remember this at the show too, for a stroke or two down the back will remove surface dust then and reward and enliven the exhibit.

Of the extra checks I mentioned just now the teeth, eyes and ears come first. Check for position if they are still coming through, and if the dog is getting on in years watch out for tartar deposits, and if you find them creeping around the base of the carnassials and back molars scale them off with a proper scaler (Nos. 3, 12, 14 and 18 I have always found to be the most useful of the set: No. 3 for the titchy bits of scale on the incisors and No. 14 for the large flakes on the molars). Eyes must be watched daily and at the first

signs of trouble bathe with a mild boracic solution or
a wedge of cotton wool soaked in ' Optrex '. Ears too
need a check over for lacerated leather, hardened wax
or just plain dirt. Sores creep about so quietly they
may appear under the armpits without notice unless
you watch, so an occasional dusting with boracic powder
there helps—and the dog cannot lick it off from there.
Vent and nails are easier still: not everyone bothers
about examining the anus but it is as well to just in
case the anal glands are swollen, or the vent itself is
sore from passing hard stools, or a segment of tapeworm
may be adhering ; and nails need watching and trimming with a fairly fine file, downwards and across,
though if they do not tend to split they can be cut
neatly with proper nail clippers . . . ample play and
walking on concrete or country roads generally keeps
them short enough.

Bathing should be done when it is necessary, and
that means when the dog is so filthy that no ordinary
grooming will remove the dirt. It sounds a bit drastic,
I know, but dogs are washed far too often to my mind,
and I think two or three baths between the spring
and autumn quite sufficient. Individual dogs will get
themselves in terrible messes, but these are exceptions,
the majority of properly controlled dogs keeping pretty
clean all things considered. Swimming in river or sea
helps to clean and invigorate the bodies, but care must
be taken to dry thoroughly afterwards. Even the so-
called ' delicate ' dogs like Whippets enjoy sea bathing (see page 395 in *Dogs in Britain* if you think it
hard to believe), but remember river water runs, and is
never so warm as the sea unless it is shallow and wide,
and the time is really mid-summer. In any case long-

coated dogs should not be allowed to swim too frequently; nor should they be allowed to play in snow if exhibition dogs.

To those of you who have just acquired your first Afghan and may think you need all sorts of special gadgets and preparations for bathing him I would say that there need be no more work in bathing an Afghan than any other biggish dog with a generous coat. The job takes a little longer than bathing a short-coated dog of the same size but otherwise there is nothing especially to worry about in the doing of it. I think it is kinder to the dog if you begin drenching and washing on the legs first, working up the body slowly so that the temperature of the body can be maintained at least for about half the time of the whole operation; shivering is thus avoided to some extent, and if the legs need rinsing even again after the head and body have been done, well, that does nothing but good. Rinsing is very important indeed, and several changes of water would not be too extravagant. A little vinegar (or acetic acid, as most of the so-called vinegars really are to-day) added to the rinsing water will help if the coat is a rather woolly one. Remember that Afghan feet will pick up all the dirty suds if you do not rinse them last of all before stepping out of the bath. And, a final tip, soap downwards, with the natural direction of the hair, and when drying towel downwards just the same too, and so avoid getting the hair tangled. As far as soap is concerned people have their own ideas and use Lux or some toilet soap: I would not advise novices to use the Hollywood smelly things though, far better a quiet and oily medium like Palmolive. When drying brush gently and fluff out the hairs keeping them well open before a low fire, never trying to dry the dog in front of a fierce fire or too hurriedly. In many cases only the feet need washing anyway.

## AILMENTS

These I have seen dealt with on a single page—and expanded to several volumes: for our purpose it is better if they take their own space whatever it may be, neither being compressed into one sentence for each ailment nor padded out until the dog needs the veterinary surgeon before you can read half way through. Therefore, I will be brief with each but long enough to give an idea of the appropriate first-aid treatment. For a really good study of dog ailments I would like to refer you to *The Book of the Dog* (Nicholson & Watson, Ltd.), wherein the ' Accident and Disease: Nursing and Treatment' section is well written by a veterinary surgeon of wide repute.

**Canker.** *Symptoms*—The dog holds his head to one side and scratches ; the ear is hot, swollen and red inside, possibly accompanied with a discharge. *Treatment*—Cleanse with cotton wool and warm boracic solution, use a canker lotion made by any of the reputable firms, improve the diet while sick, give a mild aperient, and protect the ears from scratching by fixing an ' Elizabethan ' collar made of stout cardboard, linoleum or light metal.

**Constipa-
tion.**
*Symptoms*—Obvious enough, of course,
and brought about by lack of exercise and/
or faulty diet.    *Treatment*—Increase or
correct the exercise and diet, especially the
latter, by adding more greens with a little
raw or stewed fruit like apples, prunes or
plums.  If you feel you must dose with a
medicine then better a syrup of figs than
liquid paraffin or a purge.

**Cysts.**
*Symptoms*—Obvious lameness with much
licking of the feet in between the pads and
toes.  *Treatment*—Careful examination to
discover the cause of the cyst and removal
of the foreign body inside the cyst, with a
building up of the general health to follow.
In summer many cysts are caused by grass
ears (like the awns of meadow barley) and
small thorns, and these must be extracted
with a pair of tweezers if protruding.  Another cause is the penetration of sharp bits
of flint or gravel into the crevices between
the pads, which set up soreness.  This is
most likely to occur in the road-tarring
months, and dogs should be exercised very
carefully where this operation is in progress.  For this type of cyst you hold the
foot in a tin or jam-jar of turpentine or
methylated spirits to dissolve the tar and
loosen the gravel, and bathe afterwards
with a warm boracic solution, bandaging
carefully to prevent worrying.  Add lots of
vitamin C (through carrots, tomato or

orange juice, etc.) to the diet and cut out all heavy foods and reduce exercise for a while.

**Diarrhœa.** *Symptoms*—Obvious, of course, and proof that something is quite wrong with the dog, and that he is trying to expel the poisons in the system. *Treatment*—This varies according to the ideas you subscribe to, for some breeders use kaolin or a binding food like arrowroot or hard boiled eggs, while others prefer to fast the dog and let the toxic matter rid itself, and then rebuild the dog's health after a good flushing out with an internal cleanser like garlic.

**Distemper.** *Symptoms*—Not always in this order but usually a rise in temperature, loss of appetite, eye and nose discharges, extreme lassitude, a husky cough and a disordered bowel movement. The ætiology of distemper is still not fully understood, though it is not such a mystery as Hard Pad, B.H.S., and other new-fangled perils, therefore the cures and cautions are varied. Inoculation is no certain prevention nor cure and thus has as many enemies as supporters. *Treatment*—Again it depends whether you are a believer in natural remedies or not: if you are then you fast the dog so he can concentrate on ridding himself of the poisons in the system, being isolated in the meantime of course, keep him warm and quiet, help to cleanse the digestive tracts with garlic oil, and rebuild in due course with the most digestible foods, like milk and honey and steamed fish.    Distemper is really a serious disease, and so if you are not a follower of the natural remedies method of healing then let your veterinary surgeon take charge of the dog.

**Eczema.**    *Symptoms*—A vesicular condition of the skin with some inflammation and small scales of dried skin (dead epithelium) if the form is the ' dry ' eczema.    In the ' wet ' form there are pustules instead of flakes of dead skin and these discharge. *Treatment*—As this is a constitutional disorder you need to clean out the digestive system and revise the diet completely, adding plenty of carrots (raw and grated or lightly cooked) or tomato or orange juice. A good tonic should also be given, like ' Parrish's Chemical Food ' or say ' Easton's Syrup ', but remember the latter contains strychnine and is bitter, so do not overdo the dose in mistaken zeal.    Externally the dog needs a helping agent like an ointment or powder specially prepared for this ailment by the well-known firms.

**Hard Pad.**    *Symptoms*—Diarrhœa with a rise in temperature to fever state, probably some thickening and hardening of the pads of the feet (and possibly the nostrils), involuntary crying, and some degree of paralysis. *Treatment*—Immediate isolation and very careful nursing are far more important than drugs—on no account give drugs of the sulphonamide group. Treat as for distemper but with even greater care, that is if the illness is really Hard Pad, and you have not been stampeded into thinking it is that merely because the condition is something you had not met before. This disease should really have been called Canine Encephalitis: the frequent hardness of pads detracts attention from the probable relationship it has with distemper.

**Mange.**   *Symptoms*—An intense itchiness and redness of the skin, a later casting off of flakes of scurf, loss of appetite, general condition and sleep, and eventually so severe an irritation that the dog is constantly exhausted from lacerating himself. The symptoms of the pustular variety of mange include a later eruption of pimples which discharge matter ejected by the burrowing mites which cause the illness and a swelling of the entire skin with ridged furrows and a powerful mousy smell—this pustular form is the more severe and is the worse of the follicular type, and generally has fatal results. *Treatment*—Better put in the hands of a veterinary surgeon if he is a good one and a dog specialist. Otherwise isolate the dog, burn his bedding and collar, disinfect thoroughly everything the dog has been in contact with, remove the hair from the affected parts, bathe with a solution of warm water and peroxide of hydrogen and wash with ' Kurmange ' or a similar preparation. Repeat the bathing every day for three days, rest the dog on the fourth and start again, carrying on this performance for three weeks to a month until cured . . . it really is an awful business, but rigid cleanliness and doggedness will pull him through in the end. But even when ' cured ' keep him on his own for a while longer and rebuild his condition, before letting him join the other dogs.

**Worms.** For this tailpiece I will quote the reference to worms in the book *How to Live With a Dog* (Feature Books, Ltd.): ' Tapeworms can reach a length of fifteen feet or more— but so can this paragraph if I go into details: better to copy the roundworm and squeeze into a few inches. Roundworms are the lesser evil, affect puppies more than adults, are easily expelled ; tapeworm affect all ages, have hooked heads, self-reproductive segments, and are hard to expel. The secret of expulsion lies in rigid fasting before dosing (starve the dog and you starve the worm ; it leaves its nest in the intestinal mucus, and hunts for food ; the vermifuge arrives and hits it with full force—exit tapeworm) . . . and there is no other secret at all.' And with that I couldn't agree more, except that it is only fair to the dog to add that by using the new arecoline-acetarsol for tapeworm the preliminary fast can be dispensed with. Remember there are far more dogs with worms than are generally suspected—I would go so far as to say that three of every five dogs in Britain are affected at some time or other. In house-dogs only the proportion is higher: of strays as many as 81.4 per cent are infected with worms.

# CHAPTER VIII

## EXHIBITING

Dog shows have become the shop windows of the dog world, where breeders have the opportunity not only to enter their best specimens against each other before the judges but to display their wares to the buying public. It is at the show therefore that quite a lot of business is done in sales of present stock and booking of orders for forthcoming litters, and every breeder should be awake to the possibilities in those directions.

However, the principal object of show attendance is to obtain an expert opinion on the dogs you exhibit, to accumulate awards and raise the reputation of your kennels and the particular dogs you are exhibiting, and so indirectly attract visiting bitches to your stud dogs, and finally to be in a position to breed even better exhibits. At small local shows mediocre dogs may just win something or other but the real aim should always be to enter your best dogs at the major shows and come home with the Challenge Certificate each time: let the same dog win three of these under three different judges and he becomes a Champion ... *there* is stimulus enough. Of course it is easier said than done but Champions are made time and time again—if they were not the show business would fold up right away.

## GETTING READY

Lists of forthcoming shows are published each week in the dog papers and so plenty of advance notice is given of shows to come at which your dogs would be eligible. Dates, distances and classes should be studied carefully, for then you can plan perhaps a short tour of shows in a given area with the same dogs, and in any case if you are like the average exhibitor you will not want to just throw good money away on expensive show tours unless they tie up indirectly either by location or by grading upwards to the final one of the tour. If you merely wish to try out a youngster or two then choose a local or small show, not necessarily that in your own district, and graduate to the larger shows, where the competition is hotter, later on, and drop in at a few shows and get an idea of procedure. Unless you are a regular exhibitor do not expect schedules of the shows to be sent to you without asking: most show promoters will send you a schedule once they know you are interested in their shows, but at first better ask for them.

Remember the dogs to be exhibited must be prepared for the big day, their coats must be just right, condition must be good generally, bitches must not be in season, and not only prepared for the early classes but for the open or finals too if you think they have a chance to run

H.

through the 'easier' grades.  Handling practice can be given the dogs and yourself before the time comes in a dummy ring fixed up at home: in my *Dogs in Britain* I illustrated this tip and showed how simple a matter it is ; and in any case some rehearsals are advisable where the dogs are inclined to be fidgety.  Ring practice can include not only walking round and showing off gait but the actual setting up or positioning of the dogs, and while at it rehearse trying to display the dogs' best points without necessarily hiding the blemishes.  Get the dogs used to being handled by strangers as far as is possible, and remember to keep the dog on the inside of the ring at all times, that is, between the judge and yourself where he is in full view. If the dog to be exhibited is a complete novice it is a good plan to train him to sit without being held on a home-made structure resembling show benching (or even a suitable chair) so he may the quicker behave himself when on the bench and left possibly alone for a while.  (Should he *have* to be left alone at the show do check the benching chain you took with you and see it is not long enough to let him fight his neighbour or jump down and choke, or too short for moderate movement.)  The partitions between pens at many shows are of galvanized zinc, and when chains rattle against them the clatter is enough to upset a nervous or inexperienced exhibit, so if you can get the novice dog used to the clanking chain noises then all the better.

Well before the date, if the show is far from home make sure you have booked accommodation where the dogs as well as yourself are welcome.  And also well before time send in the entries duly filled in and accompanied with the remittances (it is so simple to complete them and then forget to post the things, that you should never think of them having been attended to until they drop into the pillar box). If the show is your first then start right away listing the items you think you will need with you. If you are a regular exhibitor you will, of course, have a special case already packed with show things in. These depend on the circumstances governing the trip, naturally, but above all remember to travel light, for often the show venues are far from the nearest station or bus depot and you can stand hailing taxis until your classes are finished if you are not prepared to walk the last stage with luggage and dogs together.

A small grip containing an overall, bench blanket, brush, dog gloves, titbits, food for the dogs, bowl or plastic dish, double-hooked benching chains and show leads, toilet bag and hand towel, disinfectant, food for yourself in case you cannot fight your way to the refreshment bar, filled thermos flask, and whatever personal things you really need to add. These alone will almost fill your grip but there will be bound to be others you will probably add at the last minute. In your handbag or pocket remember your schedule, route and stud cards if any, hotel acknowledgement, show passes, ring numbers and other things.

Do not wait until the last minute to decide what clothes shall be worn at the show. These should have been selected well beforehand, remembering that you will yourself be on view in the ring as well as the dogs, and considering the type of show you are visiting. If a drab drill hall then brighten the place up a bit with something rather nice, if a big affair then go really smart, and if an open-air summer event like Richmond then dress so that you fit into the show. Some exhibitors seem to wear the same attire all the year round: this helps recognition of the wearers of course, but recognition of their dress is not always so pleasant. So wear something smart and serviceable, suited to the show you are attending, and the dogs you are exhibiting. Fluffy or frilly things should have no place in a dog show, and high heels do not exactly help in handling. But a neat costume, blouse and skirt set, slacks and shirt, divided skirt, or button-front dress all look good and allow freedom of movement with grace. Men generally have so little a variety from which to choose that they cannot help but go in suits or jacket and flannels, but often the Terrier men do not look their best, for they spoil their appearance with layers of chalk dust caked over their suits, and are sometimes really smothered in the stuff.

## SHOW PROCEDURE

Vetting the dogs should be the first thing done on arrival, and if the staff do not see your dogs are examined at once go to the veterinary surgeon yourself and get it over. In any case you should disinfect arriving at and leaving the show: at the show there are free services. The moment this is done get your catalogue, for you may not be able to leave the benches once settled there or they may be sold out later on . . . and hang on to it because a marked catalogue of a show you exhibited at in the distant past has extraordinary value when you want to study form and breeding lines. On getting to your bench fix the dogs comfortably first, check the time for your first class, and then unpack: these things all come so naturally really, but it has been known for a novice exhibitor to be so intent on unpacking herself that in the meantime the dogs have got themselves unpacked and there were many mad merry moments getting them all together again. (Incidentally, it *is* possible to go home again and forget to take the dogs with you: there was just such a case at the 1949 Birmingham National Dog Show!) So see the dogs are securely fastened on the right length of your benching chains before bothering about whether the drink in the thermos is still hot, or who else is at the show.

A little while before class time titivate the appropriate dog up to his best and let him relieve himself in the exercise yard, and then go to the ring and watch for your turn. It often happens that house-trained dogs do not at first recognize and use the exercise area as a place for attending to the needs of Nature, so in such cases encourage them to relieve themselves immediately before entering the building in which the show is held, but take them several times to the yard during the day just the same so they can see what the old hands at the show game do and learn to do likewise. As far as last-minute preparation is concerned you will still have several chances of touching up your Afghan here and there and the dog need not be strained the whole time he is in the ring but allowed to look around and settle until such time as the judge gets to the exhibits second or third along the line. Look your best and confident, let the dog look his best, and let your number display itself too—one without the others is not much use when the judge is busy.

Never talk to the judge unless asked a question, when

a prompt and brief answer should be given. For instance the judge *very* often asks for the age of the exhibit he is examining, hence the novice should have the dog's age worked out beforehand, and give it to the judge without hesitation or trimming. If in doubt about the details of procedure then ask the steward or the exhibitor next you. Move to the positions indicated when asked and not to somewhere just about the indicated place: obedience in the ring is the only place where it is needed after all, and a disciplined crew of handlers means the judging can be done not only quicker but more efficiently. When it is over leave quickly and make room for the next class, unless, of course, you are in that one too. If you have won a card in this class then better put it out of sight during the next, and the prize cards you win can be displayed above your benches where they will attract attention to your dogs and possibly induce sales of stock to visitors.

Remember that if you win even consistently at the small local exhibitions your dogs are not necessarily of excellent quality on the one hand, yet on the other hand because they may be beaten at the Championship or other Open shows they are not necessarily mediocre. In other words a v.h.c. ('very highly commended' card) at a Championship show where competition is the most keen should not be regarded as an 'also ran' award but ranked about equal to a first at a Sanction or Members' show. The beginner should really exhibit first at the small shows, but attend the important ones alone and study the exhibits there, watch the experienced breeders handling and setting up their dogs, and note especially (marking his catalogue) to whom the prizes are awarded.

If you find your group of show-going dogs consistently win at the small shows then enter them in the higher shows or try them out at a breed show. But if you find them consistently losing give them a rest for a while, for there must be a good reason for their being beaten, and try again after a rest period with fresh dogs or under different judges; always bearing in mind, however, that whatever dogs you have and whoever the judges may be your exhibits must be put down only in the best condition you can give them. The Afghan is rapidly attracting attention and therefore the rivalry at shows is pretty hectic; even in variety classes the Afghan can make an excellent display and 'enter the money'. So go in with your exhibits therefore as though you had the best of each sex on your leads but be prepared to lose with a kind heart to the best dog or bitch.

## CLASSES

In every schedule you will find a list of defined classes offered and these are taken from the official list prepared by the Kennel Club. The smaller the show the fewer classes will be offered, of course, while at the Championship and other Open shows the classes scheduled will run from Puppy to Open Dog and Open Bitch. In the list that follows here it is to be understood that the word 'dogs' applies to both sexes, and that the classes may be duplicated at any one show, one being for dogs and the other for bitches.

## DEFINITION OF CLASSES

### (Vide Kennel Club Regulations for Definitions of Classes)

**PUPPIES UNDER SIX CALENDAR MONTHS OF AGE ARE NOT ELIGIBLE FOR ENTRY**

A dog is not eligible for entry in Variety classes unless entered in Breed classes, where such classes are provided for which it is eligible.

A dog shall not obtain a Challenge Certificate unless it has won a prize in a class confined to its recognised breed or variety in which full prize money is offered and open to all exhibitors at the show in question, and unless it is in the show at the time the award is made.

In the case of a dog owned in partnership, and entered in Members' classes or competing for Members' Specials, each member of such partnership must at the time of entry be a member of such Association, Club or Society.

In estimating number of prizes won, all wins previous to the midnight preceding the day specified in the schedule for closing entries shall be counted when entering for any class. Equal awards shall count as a win for each dog so placed.

Wins in Variety classes do not count for entry in Breed classes, and a win not dependent on judging by breed points does not count. A Variety class is one in which more than one breed or variety of a breed can compete. A first prize does not include a first prize in Club Stakes or a Special prize of whatever value. With this proviso the following are the definitions of certain classes:

**Special Puppy**—for dogs and bitches of six and not exceeding *nine* calendar months of age on the day of the show.

**Puppy**—For dogs and bitches of six and not exceeding *twelve* calendar months of age on day of show.

**Junior**—For dogs and bitches of six and not exceeding *eighteen* calendar months of age on day of show.

**Maiden**—For dogs or bitches which have not won a *first* prize of the value of £1 or more.

**Novice**—For dogs and bitches which have not won more than *two* first prizes each of the value of £1 or more.

**Debutant**—For dogs and bitches which have not won a *first* prize of the value of £2 or more.

**Undergraduate**—For dogs and bitches which have not won more than *two* first prizes each of the value of £2 or more.

NOTE—No dog is eligible for entry in Maiden, Novice, Debutant and Undergraduate classes, which has won a Challenge Certificate or has obtained any award that counts towards the title of Champion under the Rules of any Governing Body recognised by the Kennel Club.

When entering for Graduate, Post Graduate, Mid Limit and Limit classes, exhibitors must count all first prize wins of £2 or more in the classes listed in the definitions whether these classes are restricted or not.

**Graduate**—For dogs and bitches which have not won more than *three* first prizes, each of the value of £2 or more in Graduate, Post Graduate, Minor Limit, Mid Limit, Limit or Open classes.

**Post Graduate**—For dogs or bitches which have not won more than *four* first prizes, each of the value of £2 or more, in Post Graduate, Minor Limit, Limit or Open classes.

**Minor Limit**—For dogs and bitches which have not won *two Challenge Certificates* or more than two first prizes in all, each of the value of £2 or more, in Open, Limit, Mid Limit and Minor Limit classes, confined to the breed, at shows where Challenge Certificates were offered for the breed.

**Mid Limit**—For dogs and bitches which have not won *three Challenge Certificates* or more than four first prizes in all, each of the value of £2 or more in Open, Limit and Mid Limit classes, confined to the breed, at shows where Challenge Certificates were offered for the breed.

**Limit**—For dogs and bitches which have not won *three Challenge Certificates under three different judges* or more than six first prizes in all, each of the value of £2 or more, in Open and Limit classes, confined to the breed, at shows where Challenge Certificates were offered for the breed.

**Restricted Limit**—Similar to a Limit class, except it is restricted to weight, colour, height, etc.

**Open**—For all dogs and bitches. If confined to a breed or variety, for all dogs of that breed or variety.

**Restricted Open**—Similar to Open class except that it is restricted as to weight, colour, height, or to Members of an Association.

**Field Trial**—For dogs which have won prizes, Certificates of Honour, or Certificates of Merit in actual competition at a recognised Field Trial.

**Brace**—For two exhibits (either sex or mixed) of one breed or variety belonging to the same exhibitor, each exhibit having been entered in some class other than Brace.

**Team**—For three or more exhibits (either sex or mixed) of one breed or variety belonging to the same exhibitor, each exhibit having been entered in some class other than Brace or Team.

# CHAPTER IX

In November 1925 when the Afghan Hound was granted Championship status the breed was already enjoying the support of its first club. This body was the old Afghan Hound Club, which has been dead for twenty years now. The application to register its title was made in the spring of 1925 and came before the appropriate committee of the Kennel Club on 17th April of that year and was granted. As I have already stated earlier in this book Miss D. E. Denyer was the principal force behind the formation of the Club, and became its first secretary, with Captain T. S. Waterlow Fox as first president.

The Afghan Hound Club was removed from the list of registered societies in 1931 but in the meantime the Afghan Association had been formed in 1927. The principal supporters of the new body were Mrs. Phyllis Robson, Mrs. Olive Couper, Miss Gwen Ide, Mrs. Eileen Drinkwater, Mrs. Rothwell-Fielding, Miss A. M. M. Simmons, Mr. Jimmy Garrow, Mr. J. Beynon, Mrs. S. Rhodes, Dr. Betsy Porter and Miss Mathews, many of whom are still active in the breed. This body functioned until the outbreak of the Second World War in 1939, when it then lay dormant until re-formed in

1945. To-day it is the principal club supporting the breed in Britain.

Sad to say the officers and their addresses change from time to time as much in this breed as in any other but at the time of adding this chapter at the galley-proof stage the present officers of the Afghan Hound Association are: president, Mrs. Drinkwater; chairman, Mr. Howard Gibson; secretary, Mr. D. G. Cooke; and the committee is comprised of Mr. Kenneth F. Parratt, Mrs. Molly Sharpe, Mrs. Howard Gibson, Mr. Edgar Abson, Mrs. Elsie Tisdall, Mrs. S. Devitt, Mrs. Riley, Mrs. K. Tziros and Mr. A. D. A. Munro. The annual subscription is one guinea.

Besides this powerful Association there are two regional supporting clubs for the Afghan in Britain, the Southern Afghan Club and the Northern Afghan Hound Society. The former was formed in 1946 and the latter in 1947. Each club has held successful shows from time to time.

The secretaries of each club at present are as follows:

AFGHAN HOUND ASSOCIATION: D. G. Cooke, Esq., 11 Reeth Road, Hartburn, Stockton-on-Tees, Durham. Tel. Hartburn 2247.

SOUTHERN AFGHAN CLUB: A. D. A. Munro, Esq., 8 Appledore Close, Edgware, Middlesex.

NORTHERN AFGHAN HOUND SOCIETY: Mrs. Ruth Y. Harrison, 36 Broxton Avenue, West Kirby, Cheshire.

# CHAPTER X

## GLOSSARY OF TERMS

**Affix.** Affixes are usually attached to dogs' registered names in order to identify them with particular kennels, and may consist of words added before or after the dogs' names. They should really be divided into Prefixes and Suffixes (q.v.).

**Apple Head.** One with the skull rounded on top as in Toy Spaniels.

**Apron.** The long hair on the throat and brisket forming a frill.

**Barrelled.** A barrelled dog is one who shows marked rotundity of the chest, having great width at the expense of depth.

**B.B.** Best of Breed. A dog who has beaten all others of his breed.

**Beard.** The attractive long hair sometimes found on the chin of the mature Afghan.

**Blaze.** A white (usually bulbous) marking running up the centre of the head.

**Bloom.** Glossiness or good sheen of coat.

**Bone.** A well-boned dog is one possessing limbs giving an appearance and feel of strength and spring without being coarse.

**Br.** Breeder, that is, the owner of the dog's dam at the time of whelping.

**Brace.** Two dogs exhibited together.

**Brindle.** A mixture of dark and light hairs giving a general dark effect, usually being darker streaks on a grey, tawny or brown background.

**Brisket.** That part of the body in front of the chest and between the forelegs.

**B.S.** Best in Show, or Best in Sex. A dog who has beaten all others, or all others of his sex, respectively.

**Butterfly Nose.** When the nostrils are mottled or show flesh colour amongst the black or brown pigment.

**C.C.** Challenge Certificate. A Kennel Club award signed by a judge for the best dog of his sex in breed at a Championship show.

**Ch.** Champion. The holder of three C.Cs. awarded and signed by three different judges.

**Character.** A combination of the essential points of appearance and disposition contributing to the whole, and distinctive to the particular variety of dog to which the holder belongs.

**China Eyes.** The less common term for Wall Eyes (q.v.).

**Cloddy.** A low and very thick-set build.

**Close Coupled.** Short in couplings.

**Cobby.** Of compact, neat and muscular formation . . . like a cob horse.

Corky.  Compact, nimble in body and mind, lively and spirited.

Couplings.  That part of the body between the fore and hind limb joints.

Cow-hocked.  A dog is said to be cow-hocked when his hocks are bent inwards, thus throwing the hind feet outwards.  A fault in any breed, even the Pyrénean Mountain Dog and present-day St. Bernard.

Crest.  The upper part of a dog's neck.

Croup.  The area adjacent to the sacrum and immediately before the root of the tail.

Dam.  The female parent of puppies.  The term is generally used but has special reference to a bitch from the time of her whelping a litter to the weaning of her last puppy in that litter.

Dappled.  A variegated or mottled colour, usually small confluent blotches of silver with tan, black or black-and-tan.  It is by no means a new colour.

Dew-claws.  The rudimentary fifth digits and claws found on the insides of the legs below the hocks, which are better removed a few days after birth.

Dewlap.  The loose pendulous skin under the throat.

Dimples.  The shallow depression each side of the breastbone.

Down Faced.  When the tip of the nose curves well below the level of the stop.

Dudley Nose.  Wholly flesh-coloured nostrils usually cherry or coffee-coloured ; quite distinct from Butterfly Nose (q.v.).

**Feathering.** The long hair fringing the backs of the legs.

**Fl. Florellen.** The term given in Germany to tiger-marked dogs.

**Flag.** The long, fine and silky hairs under the tail.

**Fringes.** A more or less general term covering the long featherings on the ears and the backs of all legs, the breechings of the hind legs, and the flag of the tail of certain breeds.

**Front.** Strictly speaking all that can be seen from the front except the head, but having special reference to the soundness of brisket and forelegs.

**Gay Tail.** One which from root to tip is carried above the horizontal.

**Good Doer.** A dog who does well without any special treatment and has thrived from birth.

**Grizzle.** An iron-grey colour.

**Hare Feet.** Feet which are rather long and narrow with the toes well separated, like those of a hare.

**Haw.** The inner part of the lower eyelid, which is well developed, hanging open and shows red in such breeds as the St. Bernard and Bloodhound.

**Heat.** A bitch is said to be on or in ' heat ' during her œstral period, when she is ' in season '.

**Height.** Usually measured perpendicularly from the ground to the top of the shoulders.

**Hocks.** The joints in the hind legs between the pasterns and the stifles.

**Inbreeding.** The planned mating of related dogs in order to perpetuate certain characteristics which

I

may be desirable, and which already exist to some extent in the blood of the dogs concerned.

**Int.Ch.** International Champion. A dog who has been awarded Championship status in more than one country.

**K.** Kurzhaar. The initial letter which appears in many German pedigrees to identify a Smooth-coated dog.

**Keel.** The absolute base of the body with special reference to the brisket. This term is generally used in reference to low-built breeds.

**L.** Langhaar. The initial letter which appears in many German pedigrees to identify a Long-haired dog.

**Leather.** The skin of the ear flap.

**Leggy.** So high on the leg that the dog appears asymmetrical.

**Level Jaws.** When the jaws are so placed that the teeth meet about evenly, neither undershot nor noticeably overshot.

**Lippy.** When the lips are developed, or overhang, more than is correct.

**Loins.** That part of the body protecting the lower viscera, between the last ribs and hindquarters.

**Long Coupled.** Long in couplings.

**Lumber.** A dog having lumber is one with too much flesh, ungainly in appearance and clumsy in action. Not to be confused with the gawkiness of puppies.

**Maiden.** In the widest sense an unmated bitch, but in exhibition language usually a dog or bitch not having won a first prize.

**Match.** A form of competition which is usually arranged more or less privately by which members of local and breed societies can meet, discuss and compare special points in specimens presented.

**Matron.** A brood bitch. One kept for breeding purposes.

**Merle.** The term for a blue-grey mixture flecked or ticked with black, uncommon except in working Sheepdogs, Cardiganshire Corgwn and some Shetland Sheepdogs.

**Muzzle.** The projecting part of the head combining the mouth and nose.

**N.A.F.** Name applied for.

**N.F.C.** Not for competition.

**Occiput.** That part of the skull at the top of the back of the head which is prominent in most of the Hound group.

**Œstrum.** The menstrual period. A bitch experiencing œstral flows is said to be 'on heat' or 'in season', that is, she is sexually excited and ripe for service by a male dog.

**Out at Elbows.** Having the elbow joints noticeably turned away from the body due to faulty front formation.

**Out at Shoulders.** Having the shoulders protruding outwards so as to increase the width of the front, as in the Bulldog.

**Overshot.** Having the upper incisors projecting over and beyond the lower incisors. (Although a fault this is much less serious than the undershot condition.)

**P.** Puppy.

**Pad.** The cushioned sole of the foot.

**Pastern.** The lowest part of the leg, below the knee on the foreleg or below the hock on the hind leg.

**Peak.** The term applied to the occiput when it is prominent, but rightly restricted to use with Bloodhounds, Basset Hounds and many Setters.

**Pencilling.** The thin, dark and elegant lines on the surface of the toes.

**Pied.** A term used for a dog having two colours in *unequal* proportions.

**Prefix.** A prefix is usually attached to a dog's name in order to identify him with a particular kennel or breeder. It consists of words added *before* the dog's name: " *Banchory* Bolo " (Labrador); " *Rozavel* Red Dragon " (Welsh Corgi); " *Sixshot* Willy Wagtail " (Cocker Spaniel); etc. Not to be confused with a suffix, in which the affixed words follow *after* the dog's name.

**R.** Rauhhaar. The initial letter which appears in many German pedigrees to identify a Wire-haired dog. This also indicates a red dog.

**Red.** Strictly speaking this is a general term for several colours, ranging from sandy-red (Australian Terriers) and red-wheaten (Irish Terriers) through gold (Cocker Spaniels) to rich chestnut (Irish Setters), copper and mahogany (Bloodhounds). In the Afghan, reds may be light or dark, but a rich red is always attractive.

**Reserve.** Usually the fourth place after judging, that is the fourth best exhibit, though it may be the runner-up in any class.

**Ribbed Up.** A compact dog with the ribs nicely placed.

**Ring Tail.** A curled tail which describes almost a complete circle.

**Roach Back.** One which arches upwards along the spine with particular emphasis about the loins (as in the Dandie Dinmont).

**S.** Sieger (fem. Siegerin). A Champion, as seen in many German pedigrees.

**Second Mouth.** A dog has his second mouth when the first or milk teeth are replaced by the second or permanent teeth.

**Second Thighs.** The muscular development of the leg between the stifle and the hock.

**Self Marked.** When a dog is of one whole colour with white or pale points on the brisket, feet and tip of tail.

**Service.** A mating. The act of copulation when a bitch is served by a stud dog. A 'free service' is one given by courtesy of the owner of the stud following an unsuccessful service for which a fee has been paid.

**Set-on.** Where the root of the tail is set on to the hindquarters.

**Snipey.** When the dog's muzzle is weak, and too long and narrow.

**Splay Feet.** Those of which the toes are spread wide apart.

**Spring.** Elasticity. Spring of rib is when the ribs are well rounded, sound and elastic: spring of back means its ability to return to its normal level after pressure away from that level.

**Stern.** The tail. A term which should be restricted to sporting circles.

**Stifle.** The joint in the hind leg corresponding to the knee in man.

**Sting.** A tail which is fairly thin even at the root, and tapers to a fine point.

**Stop.** The depression between and in front of the eyes.

**Suffix.** A suffix is usually attached to a dog's name in order to identify him with a particular kennel or breeder. It consists of words added *after* the dog's name: " Florri *of Breakstones* " (Boxer) ; " Tracey Witch *of Ware* " (Cocker Spaniel) ; " Lotus Bud *of the Congo* " (Basenji) ; etc. Not to be confused with a prefix, in which the affixed words come *before* the dog's name.

**T.A.F.** Transfer applied for.

**Tiger Brindle.** A mixture of dark and light hairs among which the dark colour forms a series of stripes or has the resemblance of stripes.

**Transfer.** A change of ownership of a dog which is registered with the Kennel Club, duly reported, paid for and recorded.

**Tucked-up.** When the loins are lifted well up, as in the Greyhound group.

**Type.** That quality essential to a dog if he is to represent or approximate the ideal model of his breed based upon the Standard desired in that breed as drawn up by a body of recognised experts: a dog which 'has type' is therefore one who though not necessarily perfect embodies much of the ideal—conversely a dog 'lacking type' is one who though possibly possessing several good points is a long way from being a living model of the ideal.

**Undershot.** Having the lower incisors projecting beyond the upper, due to a malformation of the jaws, as in the Bulldog.

Unsound. An unsound dog is one who is unhealthy, or below average in general condition, working ability, movement or character. The unsoundness may be temporary or permanent, partial or complete: a bitch after whelping is temporarily unsound by being out of coat, etc.; a deformed or unreliable dog is more or less permanently unsound.

**Wall Eyes.** Those which are parti-coloured white-and-blue, uncommon except among merle Sheepdogs and Cardiganshire Corgwn.

Weedy. Very lightly formed and lacking in substance.

Well Sprung. Well formed, with particular emphasis on chest development and spring of rib.

Wheel Back. Another term for roach back, an arched or convex back.

Withers. That point where the neck joins the body, about the shoulders.

**W.S.** Weltsieger (fem. Weltsiegerin). **A World** Champion.

**Z.** Zwerg. The initial letter which appears in many German pedigrees to identify a Miniature dog.

Z.Pr. Zuchtprüfung bestanden. A Breeding Trial Certificate.

## DIRECTORY OF BREEDERS

'*Khorrassan*' *kennels.*
Miss Eileen Snelling, Bickenhill, Woodcote Road, Caversham, Reading, Berks.

'*Kohibaba*' *Afghans.*
Stanley F. Baker, 73 Ducie Grove, Manchester, 15.

'*Kasiro*' *Afghan Hounds.*
K. Edwards, The Elms Kennels, Wickford, Essex.

'*Kuranda*' *kennels.*
B. Rothwell Fielding, Llanfaelog ty Croes, Anglesey. (International judge.) (Established 1927.)

'*Barbille*' *Afghans.*
Mrs. D. Hall, 70/70a Church Street, Preston, Lancs. Winning dogs at stud; puppies occasionally for sale.

'*El Kabul*' *Afghans.*
Betsy Porter, M.R.C.S., L.R.C.P.(Lond.), Gors Farm, Llandegfan, Anglesey. (Kennel club judge.) Exported to S. America, U.S.A., Canada, Finland, Australia, France. Puppies generally for sale. (Breeder since 1934.)

'*Khanabad*' *Afghans.*
Miss M. Niblock, Causeway House, Cholsey, 28, Berks. Typical litters by leading sires ex-winning bitches of the famous blood lines, ' Chaman ', ' Netheroyd ' and ' Bletchingley '.

'*Otontala*' *Afghans.*
Joanne Chambers, Pilgrims Way, Barsham, Beccles, Suffolk.

'*Acklam*' *kennels.*

Mrs. Howard Gibson, St. Lawrence, Jersey, Channel Islands. (St. Lawrence 75.) Breeder of Championship winners from pre-war leading strains. At stud Ch. " Mohammed Ali of Acklam " (progeny winning at Championship shows), " Abu Zaid of Acklam ", " Gebel of Acklam ".

'*Baluch*' *Afghan Hounds, Bull Terriers, Dachshunde.*

Mrs. C. E. McGregor-Cheers, 1 Ingram Road, Grays, Essex. (Tilbury 4543.) At stud " Bletchingley Badshar ", Reserve C.C., winner, son of late "Chota Nissim " ; winning bitches. Puppies generally available. Size, bone and substance.

'*Carloway*' *Afghan Hounds.*

Mrs. S. Devitt, Streat, Near Hassocks, Sussex. (Plumpton 278.)

'*Horningsea*' *Afghans.*

Mrs. M. Dods, Stoke Poges, Bucks.

'*Barbourne*' *Afghans.*

Mrs. M. F. Masters, 32 Barbourne Road, Worcester.

'*Tochi*' *Afghans.*

Kenneth F. Parratt, A.T.D., D.F.A., West End House, High Street, Royston, Near Barnsley. Exhibitor at all Championship shows. Young stock impeccable breeding for sale or export.

'*Chaman*' *Afghans.*

Mrs. Molly Sharpe, ' Chaman ' Afghans, Collin, Dumfries, Scotland. (Collin 243.) World-famous strain of black masked Hounds, excelling in type, quality, size and coat. Dogs at stud, puppies and young stock for sale.

# INDEX